Saudi Arabia is an ancien
filled with all the modern
vides. Restless and lookin
ing, two nurses traveled い ... う**ᴄᴜᴏᴏᴇ** kingdom to ply
their skills and practice close personal contact—along
with modern medical care—with people for whom slavery, buying wives, and female subjugation is just a way
of life.

Living in a culture far different from their own, they met
many wonderful people, both locally and from several
other countries, all the while walking on eggshells with
the religious police of Saudi Arabia, lest they do something, that as females, was forbidden and could have gotten them deported—or worse, thrown in jail.

Join Ramona Forrest and Judith Corcoran as they explore
life in the Kingdom of Saudi Arabia—from a woman's
point of view.

KUDOS for *Lifting the Veil*

Lifting the Veil by Ramona Forrest and Judith Corcoran is a non-fiction book that reads like a novel. It's the story of two US nurses that go to Saudi Arabia to work in a hospital there, providing medical care to the people of a country where women are chattel and have absolutely no rights. Whatever possessed them to go to such a place, I have no idea, but I can't only imagine how much courage it took. While there, they were in constant danger of being deported or arrested and jailed for things as minor as simply being in the company of a man who was not a relative. They were also at risk of being kidnapped by a Saudi man, should one have taken a sexual interest in them, and disappearing forever. Many foreign women fell prey to exactly that, and there was no one to come to their defense. I don't think I could stand to be in a place where women have so little value. But I was captivated, none the less, by chilling stories these two nurses told. The book is very well written and highly *entertaining. – Taylor Jones, Reviewer*

Lifting the Veil of Secrets in the Kingdom of Saudi Arabia by Ramona Forrest and Judith Corcoran is the non-fiction account to two RNs from the US who traveled to Saudi Arabia to serve as nurses at the King Faisal Specialist Hospital and Research Centre in Riyadh. The book gives an in-depth account of what it is really like for women in a country where being female means you are nothing more than a possession. Although the authors didn't come right out and say it, I got the distinct impression that the men in Saudi Arabia saw women as evil, a necessary evil, but an evil just the same. Women are required to be fully covered at all times and are not allowed to so much as speak to a man not related to them. While men can have sex with as many women as they want—and whether or not the men are married seems to be irrelevant—women can be put to death for adultery on such flimsy evidence as a man's accusations. And while the authors were very careful not to judge or criticize the politics of their host country, they did not downplay the total disregard for the lives and rights of women. Even those women who were not slaves—and yes, slavery is still alive and well over there—were bought and sold on the whim of a male relative. If a woman was kidnapped, even a foreign woman, in most cases, no one would lift a finger to come to her rescue. And the women accepted this as just a part of life. I found the book to be honest, blunt, thought-provoking, and downright fascinating. It made me realize how very lucky I am to have been in the US. – *Regan Murphy, Reviewer*

ACKNOWLEDGEMENTS

We wish to thank all the lovely people who permitted us entry to a country whose culture and religion was so different from our own. We are ever grateful to all those who allowed our care, and let us peek into some of their lives, their joy and sorrows, as few have ever done. For all our days we will fondly remember the people we met and cared for. What we learned, saw, and dealt with during our years spent as nurses in the Kingdom remains forever in our hearts and minds. We always wonder about and fondly remember some certain, special few who will remain in our hearts forever.

Lifting the Veil

of Secrets in the Kingdom of Saudi Arabia

by

RAMONA FORREST
JUDITH CORCORAN

A BLACK OPAL BOOKS PUBLICATION

GENRE: NON-FICTION/MEMOIRS/SOCIAL ISSUES

LIFTING THE VEIL of Secrets in the Kingdom of Saudi Arabia
Copyright © 2013 by Ramona Forrest & Judith Corcoran
All Rights Reserved
Cover Design by Jackson Cover Designs
Copyright © 2013 All Rights Reserved
Print ISBN: 978-1-626940-94-9

First publication: DECEMBER 2013

Published by Black Opal Books: **http://www.blackopalbooks.com**

DEDICATION

We dedicate this work in part to one Saudi woman we met in Riyadh at a lovely gold souk. Amazed at the perfect English she spoke, we asked her, "You speak such perfect English and have been out in the world yet you wear the mask, and cover your face, the same as all other women."

She replied, her head held high, "Yes, of course, I am a Saudi woman."

With that, we understood her love of country and culture more completely than any class could have taught us. We have never forgotten.

Translations Frequently Used

Gutra – Head scarf worn by men and boys
Thobe – Long garment worn by men in white, black, browns or gold
Abaya – Long cloak usually black worn by females
Egal – Horsehair double band over the gutra
Jiddah – Seaport on the Red Sea
Hajj – The Pilgrimage held during the month of Hijjira
Muzzein – The one who calls the prayer from the mosque
Salat – Pprayer time, 5 each day
Igama – Our Saudi passport within country
Souk – A market area, gold, silver, spices, brass, anything
Bab – Door
Butanea – Blanket
Fain? – Where
Shukran – thank you
Bint – Daughter or young girl
La! – No
Kulu youm – Every day
Mirafic – A sitter who stays with the patient
Halib – Milk
Riyal – (ree-al) Saudi currency
Hallallah – Saudi coinage
Fi allum – There is pain
Laban – Buttermilk
Bunni – Brown
Shemaze – Saudi version of a county hospital
Sidike – Potent home brew from potatoes
Harram – Forbidden
Mush quais – Not good
Fi Arabia? – Are you an Arab Woman
Hina – Here
Emira – Princess or queen
Emir – Prince

Matawa – A religious policeman
Salaam Alaykum – Hello, peace be with you
Alaykum Salaam – And peace unto you
Boma – Swahili, meaning a house
Doctura – Female doctor
Mummarida – Nurse
Fi Aman Allah – Go with God
Anna imshee – I will walk
Mafi – None
Moya – Water
Baba – Father or a male of any age
Majilis – Bringing your complaint to your king
Yemini Blanket – A thick, wildly colored blanket
Fagah – Same as truffles
Shagoul – Work
Quais – Good
Amaliya – A surgical operation
Mustashfa – A hospital
Kateer – Very much
Shamal – Sand storm
Waleed – Sons
Hegira – The Arabic calendar 11 days shorter than our Gregorian calendar

Forward

In the late 1980's Judy and I worked as nurses at the King Faisal Specialist Hospital and Research Centre in Riyadh, in the Kingdom of Saudi Arabia. Although it's been a while since we walked those hospital halls, in that closed culture not much will have changed, especially for women. Join us in our memories of those years that we cared for the ills of the people of Saudi Arabia and those who came from nearby countries for treatment. We enjoyed the companionship of medical workers from many, many countries. Memories cling of the Saudi people who touched our lives in ways we will never forget, and we often wonder what became of those we knew.

During these years the United States of America enjoyed a high status in the Middle East and we benefited from it. The people in Saudi Arabia were grateful for our care and friendly wherever possible. The cultural things we saw and experienced during our time there will not have changed much in the ensuing years. Slavery is alive and well, and women, still heavily veiled, continue under male domination much the same as during our stay in the Kingdom.

We lived with paranoia, gossip, and innuendo in a country where all is hidden and what is seen and heard is likely a façade beneath which reality is concealed. Please forgive our lack of statistics and substantive facts, but enjoy what we ourselves did, saw, heard, or were told during those exciting years spent in a mysterious country with a hidden reality.

The authors

Chapter 1

Ramona's Arrival in the Kingdom

A long row of hooded men sat high above us, looking down upon our group of new arrivals. I found it a sight that caused a chilling sensation to settle in my bones. Those strangely dressed men renewed my sense of facing the unknown, as if my group or I needed more evidence. I'd already flown half-way around the world with no sleep. I was close enough to exhaustion that only fear of the unknown and a lot of excitement kept me going.

Our group of highly trained professionals had arrived to provide American expertise in modern medical care to the people of Saudi Arabia. Did they see us in that regard, or were we just a new influx of servants or slaves who had come to serve their needs?

I had no idea about the feelings of the others in my group, but their facial features hidden behind dark glasses and the unfamiliar mode of dress on these men appeared threatening. What thoughts lay in their minds? Why did they sit up so high to look down on us? If they did it for effect, they managed to create such an atmosphere of intimidation that I had to remind myself why we were there. I said nothing of my feelings nor did any of the others, but we stayed close to each other and that gave us some greatly needed comfort.

All the men wearing dark glasses at nearly midnight had the effect of hiding the little that was visible of their heads not already covered by either a red patterned or snowy white *gutra.* They all wore a black *egal* encircling it to hold it in place. Many sported heavy beards or mustaches, further covering their faces. Gold-threaded robes covered everything else.

Those hooded, mysterious men, a daunting sight, created a strange welcome to travel-weary newcomers into this ancient Kingdom. We never learned why those men sat there or who they were.

We huddled a bit closer together as they herded us through their archaic-appearing and nondescript air terminal and through the immigration process. Little of the paperwork and shuffling about lingers in my memory, except for armed guards holding rifles at the ready. Who did they see as a threat, American medical people? Or did they see us as a new influx of slaves to be used for their comfort?

As time wore on, we came to believe that was exactly what most Saudis thought about us. Servitude as well as slavery were very much alive and well in the Kingdom of Saudi Arabia, and we were to see it in many forms.

Forgotten for the moment were our flights to Rome and the first sight of the Alps with their mantles of glistening snow in mid-August. Also forgotten was our time in Rome where we heard the startling thwack of the Imam's knees hitting the floor of the Saudia airplane we had boarded en route to Jeddah. He had called the faithful to pray for the safety of the flight ahead.

Startling though it was, it helped me realize we'd entered a totally foreign world. We learned it was the time of the yearly Hajj, and many on the plane were making their pilgrimage to Mecca and Medina, the holiest of cities in all of Islam.

Arriving in Jeddah from Rome, those worshippers who were making the pilgrimage then disembarked to journey on to those holy cities previously mentioned. We continued on to Riyadh, the capital city which was located near the center of the country.

In Riyadh, the immigration process which consisted of holding out our passports for inspection. Then we made our way through to a mini-bus with about twenty seats or so. Our luggage was piled onto a flat-rack truck that followed us as we hurtled through the night-darkened streets of the city, hither and yon.

Riyadh appeared to be a large, sleeping city scented with a lingering drift of spices and wood-fueled cooking fires, as we headed to our new lodgings. Earlier, descending from the night sky, I had noticed Riyadh, from the air, looked much like Phoenix, my home town. They both sprawled over the desert with lines of lights delineating streets laid out below us. But Riyadh streets seemed to be laid out in irregular, rather than straight rows. At two in the morning, this city of high walls lay in partial darkness except for street lights placed incidentally here and there.

Married families were dropped off first, at Sulimeniya. Single men went to another compound. When my turn came, the bus wheeled to a stop and the hooded Arab driver came to the open door and announced in an accented, sonorous voice, "Ramona Forrest, C-23." His eyes were very black, and unbelievably dead somehow. But I didn't know about that then.

His skin appeared much darker than I'd expected, and his voice was very deep and heavily accented as he read my name from a sheet of paper. It sounded rather ominous, but I recognized my name and that my lurching night-ride was through.

Did he help with my luggage? No. All four pieces lay tossed haphazardly on that flat rack truck and I had no aid in getting it off. I learned later on that a Saudi man would not assist a female, unless she was a close family member.

Tessa, another nurse from Phoenix, shared the same quadrangle, but her apartment lay across from mine. We took comfort from that small bit of closeness. Taking in the scent of smoky, incense-tinged air, we went in search of our beds. A key in the envelope of instructions became my access into dark and unfamiliar surroundings. After snapping on a light, I found a clean, neat, little kitchen; a large box of food supplies; a shiny tea kettle; and enough linens to get settled.

My new home consisted of a small kitchen, a half bath, a narrow laundry room with a stacked washer and dryer, a living room-dining room combination, all nicely furnished with Thomasville furniture, which proved to be solid and contemporary in style.

I climbed the stairway to find a full bathroom, and one unused bedroom. I took that one for mine, made my bed, and flopped down on a very firm mattress to contemplate my future in this strange country. So ended the first part of the long arduous process of uprooting my entire life. I had left all I had ever known, to ply my profession in a foreign land.

I lay there wondering. *How did I end up here?* In later years I realized much of it related to what nurses like to call, "burn out." This is a situation that occurs when things are done over and over—endless charting, lectures, diseases, complaints, settling into a daily grind. Patients are always different, but nursing retains certain similarities day in and day out that can finally cause a sense of "burn-out."

For those of us who are restless by nature, this was a well-paid chance to look over the fence and experience some exotic land far from home. To see and experience new places, and learn new things beckoned us, and I had the comfort of association with others like myself who were drawn into this adventure to experience a foreign culture.

❧❧❧

I was awakened to the multiple cries of the *muezzin* calling the faithful to the first prayers of the day. I heard—in full force—wailing sounds all across the sleeping city. The first occurred at sun-up or the first discernible light. There were five *salat* (prayer times) each day in mosques situated every three to four blocks about the sprawling city. Each mosque had a loud speaker on a tower of sorts to broadcast the prayers.

Our orientation process began that day to these mournful sounds from every minaret in the city. We were to hear this every day during our time in the Kingdom, and there was no other sound in the world to equal it. In a way, it must have sounded like air-raid sirens in London during the Blitz. It had a loudness about it, but with so many voices raised on loudspeakers all across a huge wide-spread city, a kind of softness, too.

I heard the distant wailing of Muslim prayers as I dressed. I then began my second introduction to the Middle East. A mini-bus came to take us to breakfast, and we hung on as the driver drove rapidly over speed bumps which he appeared to ignore completely.

In the hospital cafeteria, we saw the liberal use of gold leaf used on predominantly Middle Eastern paintings scattered about the walls. Gold flatware, once used in the cafeteria prior to our arrival, no longer existed. Pilfering finally put a stop to it. Yes, the authorities still cut off the hand for theft, but apparently they hadn't done it for missing flatware. I did find a gold plated spoon in the sugar canister at our apartment.

We found many choices of Middle Eastern food along with Western fare. Our group hung together, like the family we'd become. We tried the delicious looking and unfamiliar dishes, while observing the personnel presently dining. We were told that about fifty-seven countries were represented at King Faisal Specialist Hospital and Research Centre.

We saw dark-skinned Africans with bluish tribal marks tattooed into their cheeks and chins. British accents abounded. We noted they had their own particular style of eating. They held their forks and knives, one in each hand, and never transferred the forks before putting them into their mouths. It looked strange to me, but it was normal for them. Female workers from Muslim countries other than Saudi, covered their heads in Muslim fashion, but not their faces. We noticed most of them ate the British way as well.

A cacophony of voices, languages, and accents met our unaccustomed ears. I feasted my eyes on the people, modes of dress, and even the way they used their cutlery—British style for the most part. We females were properly attired in long dresses, carefully crafted at home as required. Mine was not nearly as fine or graceful as what we were seeing.

Required to apply for local identification papers, we were escorted to another office where we filled out papers for the *Igama,* our Saudi passport for identification. The male members of our group enjoyed this part immensely, since they were required to sign our applications for us. As females, we weren't allowed to do that. With a wry smile and good graces, we accepted it as a part of where we were.

A twelve-year old boy, a son of a department head, signed some of them and got a big kick out of it. His name was Ronnie and he came to love his life in Riyadh. When he had to leave the Kingdom for his education, he returned as often as possible. He left Saudi Arabia for the upper grades, as they were not given in Riyadh. His were taken in Georgia in ensuing years. I had asked his mother where he would attend school when he reached high school age.

She replied in her deep Southern accent, "Oh, in Rome."

I thought to myself, *How international she's become.* But I was deflated to learn, she meant Rome, Georgia.

We tolerated everything good naturedly since that was the spirit of things in our new life in Saudi Arabia. Lessens in behavior, protocol, and mode of dress were enhanced by warnings against fraternization with the Saudis in anything other than a professional nature. We were firmly told not to date any Saudi men.

The Saudis took our passports from us and replaced them with a brown booklet, called the *Igama.* They warned us sternly, we must not lose this identification. This new form of ID would be required to regain our passports and receive an exit/re-entry visa, when leaving the country. I felt a reluctant chill when I handed over my American passport. A thing like that is a heavily emotional experience in a strange country, but we had to do it, and we did. It helps emotionally if everyone else is required to do it, too.

After lunch, we boarded a small bus for a tour of Riyadh. Our guide was Ingrid, a woman from Germany. She pointed out the steps of the city hall. "Dot iss vere dey cut off de heads on Friday morninks." Enjoying the shock value of her speech, a sly chuckle escaped her lips. The streets, clean and free of debris, had foreign workers picking up trash and sweeping sidewalks.

Men and women walked together. The men wore traditional Arab dress. The women appeared as a black triangle of femininity from head to toe, their faces covered by several layers of black veiling. Someone remarked that the women wouldn't be able to carry much since they had to hold their *abaya* (a cloak-like cover) together with at least one hand. We occasionally saw a woman wearing a Bedouin mask with open slits for her eyes. Most eyes were strikingly beautiful, shining black, and slightly almond-shaped.

Our guide also made sure we saw a few of the many, many, gold and silver shops, known as *souks,* in downtown Riyadh. Gold of every imaginable sort lay before our eyes. There were chains, medallions, rings, bangles and bracelets. All the gold was 18-karat or above. A fabulous assortment of wonderful earrings lay before us, displayed on bright red velvet walls or in trays. In the silver *souks*, silver ornaments lay against soft, deep blue velvet, the better to display it.

All in all, we oohed and aahed sufficiently to satisfy any guide. In truth, I believed we were overwhelmed by what we'd seen, tired as we were. We would become well acquainted with these unbelievably opulent shops during our stay in the Kingdom.

Chapter 2

On the Floors

Our particular specialties spread our group from one end of King Faisal Specialist Hospital and Research Centre to the other. There was a Recovery Unit, ICU, CCU, IV Team, Medical Supply, Mechanical Maintenance, MRI and CT Scan areas.

Once on the floors, I accustomed myself to being stared at continually. Why? It was impossible to know their thoughts. But I believed the sight of a Western woman with her face uncovered, arms bare to mid upper-arm, possibly a white pant suit with the tops covering the derriere adequately, might be a sight they'd never seen before. Thus they found it of extreme interest.

I soon realized it was not unusual or offensive to have ten or more pairs of curiosity-laden black eyes fastened on you while you performed your nursing duties. Although, I was never truly certain why they observed each us so intently. I easily believed our every move held the greatest interest for them. It was likely that one reason they found us so interesting was that they were suddenly seeing females perform mysterious procedures that were not done by their women. I wondered if they wished they might do some of those things, themselves.

In their closed society, showing bare skin did not happen. It could mean death for a female, should a male, who is not brother, father, uncle, or husband, see her uncovered face or bare arms without a male family member's permission.

As we assumed the routine of our life and work in a new culture, each day brought further insight into an ancient tribal way of life. They were working to enter modern life, or at the very least, to take advantage of the wonders offered by modern medicine and financed by oil revenues.

The kingdom spent lavishly on medical care for its own people. All Saudi citizens were eligible for free services, and people from surrounding countries were invited to send their most difficult cases to King Faisal.

Outside the hospital, Riyadh bustled with new construction. Oil money was liberally spent and the effects were seen everywhere. Cranes rose into the desert air throughout the city. I frequently heard the comment that the construction cranes were called the national birds of Saudi Arabia.

Some Bedouin camps were awarded water trucks by the king. We never found out why that was merited, but with a water truck, they had their own personal oasis at hand. How far the water was hauled, we never learned, but gasoline was about twenty five cents per gallon.

Superstition and methods used for centuries conflicted or co-existed with modern medicine. The title doctor had great magic, especially if a stethoscope lay about their necks.

Bedouin burns, (our name for them) round scars, or raw, healing wounds were commonly seen in places associated with individual sources of pain. These burns were noted on Bedouins or nomads living farther out, rather than those who lived in the city. My feelings ran wild, imagining abdominal pains being treated with the glowing end of a stick thrust into fire, brought to glowing heat, and applied to that particular area. What a lovely, humane cure for an acute attack of appendicitis! We learned that this ancient method of treatment was still in use by the unlettered and more rural Bedouin tribes—another surprise in a series of many.

I was assigned to A-2, post open heart, neurosurgery, and general surgery. On this ward, I began my first experience of close association with Saudi patients. Open heart surgery in Saudi Arabia was rarely associated with clogged arteries. The usual Saudi cholesterol levels were about 125 or less, and coronary bypass operations were not the usual type of open heart surgery. The only one I knew about was a Sudanese gentleman, a chef in one of the royal palaces. Perhaps he enjoyed far too much of the rich food he prepared.

Our patients usually had valve replacements due to marrying their first or second cousins, which frequently resulted in congenital heart valve malfunctions, strabismus (crossed eyes), among other in-breeding consequences.

One of my first close encounters with an Arab male came in the form of a young boy in his early teens. He took it upon himself to instruct me in Arabic language usage. Believe me, that boy was destined to become a drill sergeant in his adult life. He pointed to a door, saying, "*Bab*." Then he pointed to bedding, pillows, a television, and anything that came into his mind.

From this boy I encountered the feeling that as a mere woman, I was subject to his domination and instruction. With humor and disbelief, I realized he saw me, a female, as a lesser being, and no doubt as his servant as well. This instruction happened every day he saw me until he was discharged. But I must say, I actually learned more of the Arabic language from him than in our scheduled Arabic lessons, which were ongoing for most of the first year.

It was no surprise to see an open-heart-surgery patient one or two days out of ICU with wires protruding from their chest, washing feet, arms, hands, ears, and any other required ablutions. Then they began the prayer, throwing down the prayer rug, and kneeling, bowing, and bending themselves in worship of Allah. They obviously had no idea of the severity of open-heart surgery. We found it interesting that it made a great deal of difference when a person knew how sick they were supposed to be, versus these people, who had no clue.

At home, a post-open-heart patient would never consider going through the same motions done by these patients at prayer. The Saudi patient does it without thought of consequence to their recent surgery. So much for restricted activity after the seriousness of open-heart surgery. We saw no adverse effects. Another item of unusual medical differences noted by American nurses was that these open-heart patients rarely received pain medication more potent than a couple of Tylenol. Stronger medication could be ordered, but was rarely required.

A female might have her operative permit signed by her twelve year old son, since she wouldn't be allowed to sign it, nor would she make the attempt. Only a male member of her family could do that, and she would never presume such a deed. Her only understanding of the procedure might be: "Cut open body and take out bad thing." We were certain that very few of our patients understood more than that.

Did they realize they were gifted by their government with the expertise of the Baylor Heart Team? Hardly. Certainly the unlettered Bedouin had little idea of medicine at that level.

Baylor kept a constant presence at King Faisal, rotating teams every four to six months. Occasionally a doctor would stay longer, joining the staff for a stay in the Middle East. On the whole, the Saudis were very grateful for the relief of pain and for curing their ills. We frequently heard them say, "s*hukran*, sister, *shukran*," (thank you) with deep, sincere feeling. The use of the word sister comes from the British and means nursing sister.

A green arrow, located in each patient room, sometimes on the ceiling, and occasionally on a piece of furniture, pointed to Mecca. Muslims faced Mecca to do their prayers, or on the occasion of death the patient was faced toward Mecca. Since the patients were in a massive structure like the King Faisal Specialist Hospital and Research Centre, these arrows were a necessity. If the need arose, they looked for it or asked, *fain, fain*, (where)? We had only to point to the green arrow.

Status was everything unless they were extremely ill. A man who had been bathed by a female nurse each day, refused to do his own bathing when he had became able. Becoming very upset, he cried, "*La, Bint toroweesh*, same, same, *kulu youm*!" (No, I do not wash, the girl wash me, same each day.) This treatment he refused to relinquish—so much for encouraging independence and self-care.

Women generally did not show their faces. An example would be a cart with a female patient passing by with a black scarf laid carefully over her face and a blanket over the rest. An Arabic-speaking female accompanied any physical exam. A doctor might deliver her baby but never see the woman's face without her husband's express permission. These happenings became the norm in our lives.

One highlight I remember well concerns a Saudi man. With a look of pride, he took his fine-looking wife by her arm and walked her carefully about the ward without a face mask. She was a woman in her thirties and she had recovered enough from her operation to need the physical exercise. She didn't look like a Saudi woman as she appeared to be taller, with a lighter complexion. Perhaps in her case, a mask was not required. While unusual, this event remained a pleasant image for me in the light of the things we'd already seen regarding the lowly status of females in Saudi Arabia.

Putting charts together, a time consuming task, had to be done. The younger Saudi patients delighted in helping with it. We laid out the different forms in the proper line-up according to the needs of the chart, and they went to it with all the exuberance of youth anywhere.

They giggled and wrinkled their noses when we wiped the tables with alcohol. Every nuance fascinated them. We had a lot of fun with these children. This meant mostly boys, since girls were too reticent if they wore the mask, and that goes on with menarche. But the younger girls, likely before their menses set in, got into the fun of putting the charts together, too.

Sometimes patients stayed with us for a longer period. Marama had an aggressive form of cancer. Her understanding of the disease was sketchy at best. Her son, a big man in his forties, acted as her *mirafic*, (sitter), though he spent most of his time ogling the nurses. Unsmiling, he sat out in the hall, watching us day and night. He ate in his mother's room and washed his clothing in the shower stall.

Marama, a small, dark-skinned, Bedouin woman with blue tattoo tribal marks on her cheeks and chin, was unable to eat. She received her nutrition intravenously. She believed the fat emulsion mixed with her nutritional solution, called TPN, (total parental nutrition), was milk, because of its white appearance. When the bottle of solution flowing into her veins got low, she would gesture excitedly, saying, "*halib*, sister, *halib!*" We made sure she never ran out of *halib* (milk).

Slavery came into our lives quietly, yet as a normal thing still practiced in this country. I saw a little black girl of six or seven, laying crossways at the foot of a three-month-old princess. It puzzled me until it was explained the girl lying crossways was a personal slave. We saw it often and, of course, said nothing. After learning that, I wondered why so many American blacks willingly embraced the faith of Islam. Their very skin color had at one time had made them a target for slavery whenever their Arab masters managed to capture someone of African heritage. It was outlawed of course, but that didn't seem to make much difference according to what we saw almost daily.

When slaves had been born and raised for many, many years in a household, where would they go if they were freed? They had known nothing else and no other life. In fairness, if a male child of a slave was fathered by a prince, the male child was raised as a prince.

The Saudi Prince, Bandar, was part African, well-educated, and held the position of Ambassador to the United States for many years. His actual parentage was not known to me, and certainly, all blacks were not slaves. Many came to Saudi Arabia for the Hajj, or holy pilgrimage to Mecca, from African countries. Finding conditions better than in their home country, they often stayed to become Saudi citizens.

We saw those we knew to be slaves, playing in the bathroom when they had a chance. What their life was like on a daily basis, we could not know for certain. We puzzled over these things often, discussed it among ourselves, and put it into the context of working in an ancient culture.

One Arab man said to me, "See that black man? My mother would say, 'Let us take him and keep him for a slave.'" This meant to me that in her time it was much more common than now. A cold chill passed over me as I heard that.

Chapter 3

The First Parties

Being new females, we were soon invited to a compound for a steak fry, dancing, and to meet and chat with Western men. I was excited as this was our first outing of the sort. Not too sure what or where their compound was, we first-timers eagerly awaited the evening.

We carefully dressed in our new Middle Eastern finery, recently purchased in the *souks* downtown. Some felt it was all right to wear western clothes covered with the black silk *abaya*. I and eighteen others, wearing the same wraps to avoid outlining our figures, were ready. We walked out to the entrance of our compound to meet our ride.

The sun had settled low in the hazy, tan horizon when Tessa and I went out to meet our ride. The dark-skinned guard was a Sudanese man whose cheeks bore the diagonal blue tribal marks. He sat in his booth, monitoring who came and went.

He didn't seem to care much if *we* came and went, but if a man drove into our housing area and didn't leave within fifteen minutes—that was different. We were to learn that some people, especially men, got a lot done within that small allotted time.

A rickety white bus sat there with the motor running and we lined up to enter. I couldn't help seeing the comparison of ourselves to black-feathered Minorca hens entering their coop as the sun went down. The bus vibrated slightly beneath our feet, while the engine kept the air conditioner blasting enough cool air to make life livable this September in the Arabian Desert.

We all wore the *abaya* in keeping with protocol taught us in orientation. We also were clothed to the wrists, ankles, with no décolletage, and no outlining of the body with belts or tight clothing. All *abayas* were black, sometimes of heavy, smothering rayon, or light, thin, silk ones with elegant lacy borders that had the effect of floating gently about you as you walked. That sort became my favorite, and I felt quite elegant floating along in one of those with a wild flamboyant border-printed, long skirt showing beneath the austere coloring of the *abaya*. I happily wore gold, strappy sandals. They made my feet look good and it wasn't a sin to wear them.

Tessa, my new friend from Phoenix, and I sat together while others sat with friends or roommates. The driver, a dark-skinned Pakistani, revved the engine and we soon wheeled about strange streets in the noisy, rumbling bus.

We were fascinated by the passing scenery outside our windows. The streets of Riyadh teemed with activity. Cars, usually parked parallel, were often parked with the front wheels up on the sidewalk and the back wheels in the gutter. We thought it hilarious, but automobiles were rather new for many of these people, and oil money appeared to be plentiful. Obviously, it took a while for people used to desert travel on camels to accustom themselves to the vagaries of modern city traffic and parking regulations. The streets of Riyadh were wide and often tree-lined with generous sidewalks. The word Riyadh means garden, and it can also be a man's name.

People walking about presented a fascinating parade of many cultures and manners of dress. In addition to Saudis who dressed mostly in white, black, or tan *thobes* (their long dress-like outer garment), with which they wore red or white head dresses with the encircling *egal*, we saw people who appeared to be a mix of, Pakistanis, Indians, Africans, Orientals, and Westerners. We could only guess where the rest might be from.

Arabs wore traditional dress more in Riyadh than other large Saudi communities, but some wore business suites as well. Arab women in Riyadh were always masked and wore the *abaya*. No Saudi female would be seen alone. They would always be with a male family member, another woman, or a group of women.

We seemed to travel forever on that rattling bus. Our destination, The Vinnel Corporation Compound, lay on the outskirts of the city. As we bounced along, a man in his late forties stood up, introduced himself, and welcomed us. He requested that after we arrived, we seat ourselves, not more than two ladies to each table so our gentlemen hosts might come and sit with us. He said they were eager, not only to talk with women, but for news from home. Their interest lay in The States mostly since our hosts were retired American military men. Their mission in Saudi was to teach the Saudis the art of developing an effective military defense system.

Reaching the compound, we turned off the highway onto a long tree-lined drive until we came to a large cluster of housing and administrative buildings. We climbed out to be greeted by numerous male voices and warm handshakes. They quickly ushered us out of the heat into a large, air-cooled room, furnished with tables and chairs.

Tessa and I dutifully sat, two ladies to each table. We enjoyed cool refreshments brought to us by polite, neatly groomed gentlemen. Shortly, after a few conversations, we lined up to receive steaks with all the trimmings. We were joined in dinner by three gentlemen. They were friendly and wanted to talk, perhaps because we were women, perhaps to hear what was happening at home or in our own lives. Sports news was important to many, but out of my sphere of interest.

They told us about themselves, their lives in the country, and shared some of their frustrations in training nomadic desert men in modern combat and defense techniques. More than one man shook his head, wondering if they were getting anywhere in their endeavors.

One man offered this comment: "They do okay until prayer time. I guess that works if the other side does the same." He chuckled about it but it made me wonder what their airline pilots did while flying.

Few of the men had families with them so they were hungry for the company of women. Some looked for liaisons and readily found them among these ladies newly unleashed from the conventions of home.

Later, we danced to the very decent music of a Filipino dance band. A Saudi man, wearing his white *thobe* and red *gutra* headdress, made me feel uneasy. I wondered if he might be spying on us. Was he curious about Western women, or did he just want to join in the fun? What was to become my continual feeling of a vague sort of paranoia, common to many ex-pats (ex-patriots) had already found a place in my mind.

Dancing with a Jordanian man in Western style dress, I was treated to the overwhelming scent of male body odor, fresh and sharp. Hairy legs on women and body odor on men seemed to be the norm there. I couldn't think of many Americans, male or female, who would adopt that form of personal care.

We stayed until about 10 p.m. and were taken back via the same bus. It was our first outing, and some of the girls had made alliances. But for me, the reality of dating a man, working and living in this country, had yet to become a part of my thinking. We weren't supposed to be seen with a man who was not our father, son, brother, or close male relative.

Paranoia comes easy when just the act of talking to a man, who isn't related to you, could cause you to be sent home. It didn't take long before that became an integral part of our thoughts.

After four years, I returned home to The States. I continued to look about me for quite some time until I realized what I was doing and broke the habit. After those years in Saudi, I had learned to be aware of who watched me or overheard what I was saying. I had learned paranoia from living in a country where people were not really free.

A Saudi man I will call "The Arab," once said to me, "Americans are not thinking bad." By that he meant we were not suspicious of other people. We tended to believe everyone in the world liked us. We seldom thought anyone wanted to cause trouble for us and, consequently, we were rather trusting souls. In reality, few other people of this world were so trusting. Of course, this sort of thinking on our part pre-dated September 11, 2001.

A tall redhead from Florida, one of our original group, had the habit of saying, "What's the worst they could do to us?" She had left her young children with relatives and was totally ready to roll. I don't remember how long she stayed, but she definitely did a lot of rolling while in Saudi. The last I heard, she had traveled around the world with a gentleman she'd met in Riyadh.

The next party came along soon after. Someone always knew where a compound held a celebration of one kind or another, and it usually happened when they had a new batch of brew ready. They let someone at Faisal know and the signs were discreetly posted about the hospital. Everything was word of mouth or discreet notes. If the Saudis knew about these clandestine get-to-gathers, they looked the other way.

Where this particular party was held, I never knew. We were driven by men none of us knew for what seemed like a long distance. I took comfort from being with others like myself and relaxed. Finally, the small bus came to a high-walled villa and drove inside huge iron gates.

By now we knew if we didn't get back to our compound by midnight, we had to stay the night and return during daylight hours. How ridiculous was that? What a set-up for meeting other ex-pats. I met many new people at this party, including one woman who wrote stories— not about her experiences in Saudi, but general fiction. A missed opportunity, it seemed to me. We ended this night staying over in makeshift beds. Our hosts made us feel our presence was precious to them.

An Italian man, imported from The States, complained bitterly and often about his accommodations. Marco felt he'd been misled about everything and went on and on about it. Trying to placate him, I asked if he hadn't had any orientation, and what had they promised him in the way of housing? He never became even partially mollified about those things, but he did become interested in me.

He had a car and, eventually, Tessa and I traveled all over Riyadh with him looking at things, bargaining in the *souks,* shopping in the malls, and eating out in restaurants. None of this was allowed by the Saudi Government. They could never imagine that a slightly older woman, being seen with a man, wouldn't be married to him. It wasn't in their thinking.

The Arabs were superb bargainers, but not better than Marco. Totally amazed at his prowess in getting his way bargaining in the *souks,* I realized it must be a way of life with Italians, too. Once while haggling over the price of a clock, Marco put a few *reals* on the counter and slowly dragged the item toward himself. When the Arab said nothing—it was Marco's.

With Marco, Tessa and I often ate in places frequented only by Arabs. The napkin—very often a roll of toilet paper with the cardboard core removed, the tissues was pulled out from the center as needed.

We tried rolled grape leaves with nutty lamb stuffing inside, Arabic bread with hummus, and spicy meats I wondered at, nor sure if it was goat, lamb, or camel. At times I sensed that some Arab men resented the presence of a Western woman in their midst. Usually a restaurant had two sections, one for men, and one for families, but not always.

We had magical fun, but things never stay the same. Marco received orders to report to the Empty Quarter soon with his company for communications installations in that region. We decided to take a trip out of the city before he left the area. A thing like that requires governmental permission and, for me, hospital permission as well. We both knew it would never be granted.

Chapter 4

On the Wards

At work we saw, along with the usual diseases, others strange to us. Shistosomiasis, a disease contracted from infested water, takes more than one form. About the worst case of this is called Bilharziasis. A man Hamid, owner of a large flock of goats, had been infected for years with some form of Shistosomiasis—during which time, several large, globular growths, formed inside his abdomen, liver, and lungs. Some of these growths were as large as a grapefruit with a thin, fragile, and rather brittle outer crust. In surgically removing these, the doctor had to exercise extreme care not to rupture the outer crusty tissues of the tumor, because the inside of the growth contained particles of dead worms.

Should these particles reach the patient's blood stream, he could suffer severe anaphylaxis. (An extreme allergic reaction which can kill within minutes by severely restricting respiratory pathways.)

Most of the waters in the Middle East are infected. A doctor told me, "If you put your hand in infected water, you might have one hundred hits by microscopic larvae in about one minute." The Nile River in Egypt is heavily polluted, according to what a doctor told me as we rowed a boat across that river. Watching kids splashing and playing in the Nile, I remarked about how healthy they looked. She informed me, "They are *all* ill from infestations in the water. Almost any pond or body of water in this country is contaminated."

She further explained that in most Middle-Eastern areas, spraying with DDT, said to be the most effective against so many parasites, has been outlawed for years. Because of this ban, untold numbers of people have died because of the diseases the pesticide might have eradicated.

Many poor, infected souls often presented (came in) with swollen livers, or wherever the invading larvae finally settled into their bodies. These patients were difficult to treat and communication about their condition severely limited.

Hamid, in particular, lingers in my mind. He was usually a happy. jovial man, in spite of his condition. He was in constant severe pain after surgery from his swollen, tender, abdomen, Hamid would cry in a squeaky, voice. *"Fi Allum, sister, fi Allum!"* Basically meaning, "There is pain, sister, there is pain." The man, not really a complainer, suffered real agony during his healing process, and we medicated him as needed.

As he regained strength, his voice returned to normal. He eventually went back to his environment, no doubt to become re-infected. I hoped we had given him a few more good years and relief from his life of misery.

෧෩෧

We continued with our Arabic lessons and, at no other time in my life, have I been so sleepy. In spite of getting some much-needed rest, I slowly learned some of the language. Each floor made it a practice to have Arab speakers present in whatever capacity, usually as unit secretaries, or nurses of Middle Eastern extraction. They always doubled as interpreters. As a last resort, we had the international telephone operator act as interpreter. The patient would relay his message to the operator. The operator would tell us what he said. As time passed, we became proficient enough with sign language, and a few hackneyed words of Arabic, to detect many problems.

On beginning a shift, we gathered in one room for report. We received the taped information (of the patients from the preceding shift) in English, as spoken by Ethiopian, Arab, Irish, Scottish, French, English, Scandinavian, African, Austrian, Australian, or Chinese. One of my major regrets has always been that I didn't snitch one or two of those taped reports. They were priceless.

As my first year came to a close, a new nurse, Judith Corcoran, came onto our floor. In my first chat with her, I said, "Judy, I'm about to go on leave for a month and I feel sorry to have to leave you here with these British nurses. They are really tough." But I happily went on my first leave home, and she managed to survive in spite of our charge nurse. The head nurse of this floor, Chang, was a Chinese woman from Singapore, who immediately took notice of Judy.

A tough boss, she definitely resented our higher pay scale compared to hers. Judy as an American LPN, received a higher wage than Chang, and the woman never let her forget it. She literally hounded Judy, looking for mistakes or any sign of a deficiency, something— anything, she could berate her with. She never really caught Judy in any wrong doing, but she certainly kept her in a state of continual guardedness.

Chang's husband, a gentle, mild-mannered Filipino man, seemed so different. We often wondered how they managed in their marriage, though they seemed happy enough together.

All reports, records, orders, and communications were done in English. Those who worked with patients or in medical fields were required to speak and understand English. The launderers, cooks, gardeners, and general laborers were not required to speak English. We saw many dark-skinned men with tribal markings (bluish tattoos) on their faces working as maintenance men and gardeners. We learned they were African, usually Sudanese whose national language is Arabic.

Once on the way to my apartment, I noticed several tribal-marked workmen covertly watching a pale-skinned Swedish woman, sunning nude in her tiny backyard. Though totally enthralled by the local scenery, they quickly scattered upon seeing me.

ودى

A patient we'd had for a long time had a sad medical history. Mohamed Taki was about fourteen years old. His brother, Abdul Hadi, had left the comforts of his wives to spend more than two years with his little brother as his *mirafic* (sitter). Abdul Hadi, while not the brightest star in the heavens, was certainly a devoted brother. He stayed through Mohamed Taki's numerous operations and became familiar with the staff and the routine.

He spent much time hanging over the nurses' desk, his lower lip drooping, and his curiosity evident. He did this somewhat more than the other visitors and *mirafics*. He followed us, making rounds with the treat cart. Most of the patients did not select the cakes or cookies, but asked for *laban,* (a buttermilk, or yoghurt), or fruit. Abdul Hadi came to like chocolate ice cream and always asked for *bunni,* (boo-nee) meaning brown. He had it often.

Sadly, the day came when the surgeon told Abdul Hadi, "I cannot fix Mohamed Taki." The boy, though very young, had a *malacia.* It was a condition that caused his intestines to become hard and rubbery, much like semi-cooked pasta. They continually leaked a yellow-tinged serous fluid and could not absorb enough food for the boy to live.

This condition, unknown to us, may have been caused by inter-marriage, or some intestinal bug, but we never knew what had caused his illness. Accurate histories were usually difficult to obtain.

Abdul Hadi cried for his brother's sake and thanked the doctor for all he'd done. The patient was either sent home, or worse, to Shemaze, their version of a county hospital. We felt defeated by this case, but it wasn't the only defeat. We had many others along the way.

About the worst case, for me personally, was the man from Yemen who had chewed a weed called *Gat.* Normally, seeing a malignancy like his, the doctors didn't admit them to Faisal. They were sent home to die. *Gat* is a narcotic plant they chew for relief of hunger, or just because they like the way it makes them feel. It has the effect of causing malignancy in some people and Fouad became afflicted. He was admitted with a small fleshy growth protruding from his right nostril.

They did what they could to treat him and, about two months later, he was re-admitted to our ward. The tumor had grown to the point that the man's nose had flattened almost across his face. His mouth and nasal passages had filled, and the odor of his destroying cancer was beyond belief. He could scarcely breathe, even with oxygen, or see out of his eyes. His brother, Naif, stayed with him, living in the room.

We used wintergreen to mask the odor. Even though we used plenty of it, spread around the room, it was not effective enough to relieve the stench of death. An exhaust fan blowing out the window helped some, too. His last days as my patient were as close to hideous as I ever want to see again, or be involved with.

His brother was to take Fouad's wives for his own after Fouad's death. I didn't hear how many wives that amounted to, but we all discussed it and decided it made for a sensible sort of social security for widowed women and children. They would be cared for.

The people of Yemen are very poor, having no oil to sell, but they do manage to survive. It's understandable that they might need relief from the pangs of hunger and that *Gat* is a sizable crop in that country.

Chapter 5

An Illegal Adventure

I gnoring the impossible, and in the spirit of adventure, Marco and I set out for Dhahran, which is on the Persian Gulf. We laughed at trouble. After all, being sent home to the United States was not the worst fate in the world. Not for me, perhaps, but for Marco, I didn't know and he never said.

We turned onto the highway and drove endless hours through the shimmering desolation of the Nafud desert. Camels grazed at tufts of long, stringy lengths of tough-looking grass that seemed to sprout out of conical mounds of sand. The lumbering camels often crossed the highway, slowly, leisurely, scraping their hind legs as they crossed over the guard rails. I wondered if they were wild or belonged to some nomadic Arabian tribe.

The sky in Saudi is rarely blue, but rather a sandy-colored, hazy mix with a clear azure blue only visible in the highest reaches of the sky. Very little seems to grow on it. How people had survived for centuries in an arid desert like this was beyond imagining. Having not yet seen an oasis, I could only wonder about it.

Along the side of the road, we noticed a flat-rack truck sitting there with four Arabs dressed in rumpled, stained *thobes* and *gutras* standing at the back of it. They looked at a small truck which had rolled off the back end, leaving the back wheels on the big truck and the front end straight down onto the gravel. This placed the body of the smaller truck, perpendicular to the ground. They had a very difficult dilemma, and we both wondered what they could do about it. It seemed they hadn't a clue about it as we zipped by in our car.

Nearing Dhahran, I heard Marco murmur, "For thees, I reesk everytheeng." With more than a tremor of apprehension, we pulled up to a Ramada Inn and, after carefully looking things over, he decided not to risk trying for a room. We drove into Dhahran and searched about the city for the right place. The Intercontinental Hotel appeared on our right, very large and impersonal. We also knew the Matawas (religious police) weren't quite so rigid in policing their faith in Dhahran.

The restaurant bustled with diners of all sorts in many modes of dress. We took a table, ordered dinner, and ate. While I sipped my coffee, Marco rented a room for a single gentleman. Much later, with the one bag taken up, he returned and casually sat a while, telling me the floor and room, then left. I waited a while then casually edged toward the elevators.

Once in the room, all was well until morning came. I didn't use the shower cap because a man wouldn't have done that, and I only used the one towel. Talk about paranoia, the whole thing seems hilarious, looking back on it, but at the time, it was nigh on to robbing a bank and risking a beheading.

Next morning, Marco took our bag down, paid the bill, and got his car. I watched furtively out the window until he waved a small, unobtrusive wave. I quietly left the hotel as if I had been taking a leisurely breakfast in the restaurant and walked out the door.

We had a good laugh when we were safely away, but we both felt the danger of breaking the laws of our host country. It actually became rather routine after a time. To free thinking Americans and Marco, too, the many ways to disobey certain laws were endless. We felt no guilt circumventing laws and customs that seemed overly restrictive to us.

We drove back to Riyadh as the sun set. More than once, we were treated to the sight of a row of Muslim men standing together facing Mecca. They performed their prayers to Allah as the sun faded away behind the distant mountains. That beautiful sight remains in my mind. I have always felt after seeing those sights, that a man facing his God is an awesome thing to behold.

I saw Marco only a few times after that, whenever he was able to return to Riyadh. He never stopped complaining about his treatment at the hands of the Saudis, the poor accommodations, the poor food, and so on. He told me about working in the *Rube al Khali*, the Empty Quarter. It was a nearly uninhabited place with endless expanses of red sand dunes, few roads, little water, and rarely any rainfall.

He had to pass over the same road many times each day, and the man who guarded the station on it made him produce the same paperwork each time. Marco found it frustrating and exasperating. He believed the Arabs enjoyed it to the max. It often seemed to us that their life was one of extreme boredom. A chance to beleaguer a foreign worker likely became choice entertainment.

Chapter 6

Life in General

Working with international people was an education in terms as well as a multitude of attitudes, mores, and values. What I might think of as a dicey situation would be met with, "What of it?" and a shrug. I had to rethink many things and found myself undergoing a quiet metamorphous.

We worked forty-four-hour weeks and spent most of our time either going to work or coming home. In my present living arrangements, I became uncomfortable with my Belgium roommate, Aneke. Maybe at this point I wanted to be near Americans, or it may have been her European outlook of obvious paranoia towards people, fellow workers, Saudis, and events. The other occupant of that house was on holiday, and I never met her until much later.

My friend, Tessa, from Phoenix, had lost her Filipino roommates to a new complex just opening. I asked if I might move in with her. She was happy to have me join her and the remainder of my four years in Saudi was spent in that house.

A request from housing was all that was required and they were eager to comply with our wishes. Before leaving, I vacuumed the former house, and Aneke thanked me for '*hoovering*'. This was only one of the new terms we were to learn.

After attending a few parties, it became obvious that you could behave in any manner you were comfortable with and do anything, short of a criminal act. No one cast disapproval in your direction. It took a while to realize you were now in a situation of almost total freedom regarding your personal behavior. I found it a strange phenomenon in a country so lacking in such freedoms.

Women dated madly, broke up, or had someone leaving, never to see them again. When their term of employment was up, they left Saudi Arabia to take up their normal lives in the real world. Heartbreak and tears were quickly replaced with the excitement of meeting someone new.

Drinking, something I never did in The States, became nearly unavoidable in Saudi. Everyone brewed some ungodly mess or other, and your approval was definitely required when you entered their compound.

"Just look at the clarity!" or, "What do you think, doesn't this beer have great body, and flavor? We just finished a batch, and we're throwing a party." They might urge, "How about a crème de menthe?" This would be the green crème de menthe liquid poured into a glass of potent home brew, called *sidike*.

This drink, not unlike grain alcohol, was made with potatoes and who knew what else? They offered red wine, that would be red grape juice with *sidike* mixed into it, and white wine, nearly the same. Compliments were generously handed around as you quietly choked the stuff down.

Every compound, to my knowledge, continuously made booze, and parties were thrown whenever the liquor supply reached critical mass. Every grocery store was heavily stocked with pressure cookers, red and white grape juice, yeast, sugar, and potatoes. The Saudis seemed more than willing to supply anything that could be utilized to meet the Westerners' demands. How could the Saudis not know what those supplies were used for?

They warned us against taking a regular Saudi Taxi cab where the driver would be an Arab wearing the traditional dress. "Only take a limo," they said. If one lone woman gets into an Arab's taxi, he can do whatever he wants to with an unaccompanied female. If there are two or more women, no problem."

We were all very careful about riding in those cabs. Most of us quickly got used to the bus system, an adventure in itself. At least at Faisal, we had the freedom to go out and take a bus whenever we had the time or inclination. I learned this was not the case at other hospitals.

The city buses in Riyadh are equipped with two doors and two sections. The first and larger section is for males. The back of the bus seats fewer passengers, and is walled off from the male sector. We rode often with Arab ladies, black clothed and masked. I can't remember any of them ever putting in a riyal or two for bus fare as required. We didn't blame them one bit. No Pakistani bus driver would dare to question one of those ladies about paying her fare, and none ever did.

We usually put in a few coins so the bus driver could hear the clink. We retrieved them as soon as they jiggled out of the bottom of the coin box. We tried chatting with the lady passengers and found them very merry and pleasant to spend time with. Often, little boys peered through the cracks from the front section to get a look at us and giggle in their naughty little boy way—little voyeurs every one. Grown men might sneak a look, but pride prevented anything overt.

Two doctor's wives entered the bus wearing short skirts and showing bare legs. We felt embarrassment for them and wondered what orientation they had received. To us, it was not right to flout the Saudi traditions. We were guests in their country and dressed and acted as required, at least in public. Those wives really missed the magic of being in Saudi Arabia. They didn't meet the so-called, every-day people. We met wild-eyed Bedouins off the desert and people who came from all parts of the Kingdom. We cared for royalty as well as the poorest soul if he needed the level of care available at Faisal. Every citizen had the right to free medical care. We were certain it was paid for by oil revenue. The universities were free as well.

Our apartments had cable TV, but nothing came on until noon. All of the TV programming was in English, broadcast from our hospital, and had been carefully edited for offensive materials. Some Arab or ex-pat had to sit through endless hours of old TV series looking for the forbidden, a low neckline, thigh, or heavy kissing. Some of the language got through because of the difficulty they had knowing exactly what was said or meant.

About the best thing we saw on TV depicted the opening of a new Saudi Military facility. During the presentation they played a nice, lilting American song. "It's a Heartache. Nothing but a Heartache." The news most often depicted visiting dignitaries kissing the King and being kissed. Yasser Arafat visited very often and we deemed him about the ugliest man in the Middle East.

Visiting the markets held a few surprises as well. When *salat* was called, huge drapes covered the front of the store, all check-out counters closed, and the Faithful went to prayer. We were allowed to continue with our grocery shopping in the eerie quiet of prayer time. We were allowed to enter the store through the drapes, so we could get out of the heat, and do our shopping.

On one of these tours to the A&P, or the Al Azzia Market, a man kept following me about the store. I noticed he frequently rubbed himself near his privates. Finally, he found the courage to ask, "You come my house, I bring you right back."

Incensed at his request, I fired back, "*La*! *Harram*! *Mush Quais*!" meaning, "No! It is forbidden, No good!"

The man looked desperate, but he left and I didn't see him anymore, thank God. It was scary, though we laughed about it later. We wondered if because I was an infidel in his eyes, I was merely one more Western woman of easy virtue? They generally thought that of us if we were not Muslim.

We went by bus everywhere: to the Euromarche, Al Akaria Mall, the brass souks, downtown, Al Batha District, the Glass Mall, and no one ever accosted us. We saw falcons sitting, hooded, on their perches, their sharp beaks gleaming in the sunlight. Bedouin women sat about with slotted masks, that revealed their beautiful black eyes, as they sold pots in the brass *souks*. Many people casually tossed wrappers and debris on the streets. The foreign workers kept the streets clean. Everything interested us, including the skinny little man from Yemen toting a refrigerator on his back.

On one outing with my friend, Jamilla, who was a mix of American and Iraqi, a man asked her, "*Fi Arabia?*" meaning, are you an Arab woman. He said this as he gazed into her wide green eyes.

She replied in Arabic that she was of both cultures. He told her, "You have the beauty of the East and the beauty of the West." It was all in Arabic, of course, but she told us what he said and had a giggle about it. We had much more freedom than workers in any of the other hospitals.

Chapter 7

A Visit to a Palace

One morning they called me to the nursing office. One of the royal princesses needed nursing coverage, during the absence of her live-in British nurses. It seemed that one was leaving on holiday and one was returning. Though hesitant and a bit fearful, I said I would do it. I came to this country for the adventure of nursing in a foreign country, and this would surely be it.

From stories and movies, most people have an idea what a palace looks like. I had seen them in movies, only. If the lady was a princess, it followed that she would live in a place like that. Silly me.

Right or wrong, being an American gives one a feeling that everything will be okay, a sort of inner confidence. After all, trusting souls that we are, as the Arab said to me "Americans are not thinking 'bad,'" we trust most everyone.

I packed a small bag, wore my ID badge, a stethoscope, and long street dress covered with a silk abaya. I waited at the gate of our compound. The palace doctor came for me. A Pakistani man, he spoke some English.

Now I will see the palace. Exciting thoughts roiled about in my head as we drove. As we entered another section of Riyadh, it quickly became apparent that there was not one palace, but literally hundreds scattered all about. They were everywhere. One palace had been constructed to emulate our White House. There were five thousand princes at the time, and it looked like each one had a palace and a regal one at that. (Oil money.)

Reaching this particular palace, we entered through an eight or ten foot wall, past huge iron gates, and into the beautifully landscaped domain of royalty. This compound comprised more than five acres overall. Smaller buildings were set against the outer walls. There were several imposing marbled houses.

Each wife is entitled to a residence of equal value and, in our travels about the city, we had frequently seen three or more very nice residences and a more sumptuous one for the Prince. In this particular compound, I saw three large marble houses at least two stories high. I do not recall seeing the house of the prince. Along the insides of the high walls surrounding the entire compound were buildings, housing, and shops. Trees, shrubs, flowers, and grass grew in profusion, softening the landscape, making it a lush paradise in appearance.

The doctor ushered me into one of the three, equally set-up dwellings. It had to be the home of one of the wives of a prince. A large home, it was made of beige marble. I was led up a wide curved stairway of the same marble. There I met Kelly, a British nurse leaving on holiday. She explained that Liz, another nurse, hadn't returned as yet, which was my reason for being there. Kelly had kindly written out detailed instructions for me as to medications, dosages, times, and other requirements in caring for this princess.

The family name was Al Saud. To me, that name meant the patient was closely related to the royal family. Her medical history was a poor one that proved to be a long, painful, Murphy's Law of medical problems. One problem had led into another, finally leaving her in need of constant care, with a carefully programmed rehabilitation regime, done by skilled personnel.

After introducing me to the patient, Kelly left for the airport. I felt bereft at first. My Arabic was poor at best, and deciphering the princess's immediate needs was a bit difficult. Her maid kept close attendance and spoke a few words of English, which eased things somewhat.

After a longer time in the Kingdom, I learned that the dark-skinned maid was a slave woman. She slept crossways at the foot of the princess's bed. I was to see this frequently during my four years in the Kingdom.

How did I learn this? One day, we had a 3 month old princess as a patient. A small dark skinned child of eight or ten lay on a padded blanket placed crossways at the foot of this baby's crib. I asked the why of this and learned the answer. "She is the tiny princess's personal slave. The identifying key is that they lay crossways at the foot of the bed."

This Al Saud princess had a daily routine which was rigidly maintained during my stay. She slept until ten each morning and went to bed about eleven each evening. Her personal maid (or slave—I hated the word) gave most of the personal care, bathing, and dressing. She needed assistance with getting in and out of her wheelchair and transferring to her chair in the sitting room. I helped her with that when I could, though medications and overseeing her care was why I was there.

During the afternoon and evening hours, the princess entertained female friends and family members. She had a very large sitting room, with a couch that easily held five or more. Each room I saw was sumptuously furnished with silks and damasks, draped in the finest of window coverings, and with solid, finely crafted furniture. In that home, I saw fabulous furniture I never knew existed.

Once each evening, she was wheeled across the hall by her woman to an identical luxury apartment to visit her mother. There she sat with visiting females whose royal rank I never knew. This was her daily routine, and it never varied. They sat there and drank tea, ate sugared dates, cookies, and imported Belgium chocolates while they chatted in Arabic.

I was responsible for giving her medications and requesting needed supplies and medicines. I had only to ask the doctor and he was quick to grant any request made of him. This obvious subservience made him more of a flunky than a medical doctor, to my mind.

During mealtimes in the princess's apartment, I was served on the kitchen floor. The royals or visitors ate on the living room floor, except for the princess who could not do that. She remained in her chair, and her mother or her slave assisted her with eating. I did her medications and wondered if, as an infidel, I touched something she ate, would she think it harmful in some way?

Of course, we had been taught that we hand meds to a patient with our right hand. The left hand is kept for personal cleaning, and thus is considered unclean. It is a grave insult to an Arab patient to hand them medicines with the left hand. We were careful to abide by this rule.

The food came on a silver tray with fine china dishware and gold-plated flatware. My dinner consisted of lamb, chicken, a fried goat brain, three kinds of vegetables, a pasta dish, Arabic flat bread, salad with no dressing, and fruit for dessert. My food was excellent and of the same quality as the princess. (I didn't try the goat brain.)

The princess's condition required routine physical therapy sessions which she continually refused. They were painful and, as a princess, perhaps she didn't wish to endure the suffering caused by this therapy. This is what Kelly told me.

About eleven PM we assisted her to bed. To be within earshot should she need me, I slept on a thick padded comforter called a Yemini blanket. It was folded into a soft mat just across the hall from her door. There was a nice breeze flowing across me which made the whole unbelievable scenario rather pleasant. I fell into a deep sleep. When she called, I roused enough to attend her before returning to my own slave bed.

The surroundings of the place seemed opulent and extravagant to my eyes. But when people keep a million American dollars stowed under their beds, just in case—maybe not. The dining table could have easily held twenty. It was of heavy dark wood, with lovely carved chairs to match. I never saw that set used. They seemed to eat on the floor for the most part and I wondered if that dining set had ever been used at all. That lovely furniture, seen but rarely ever used, implied her status.

In the kitchen, the latest in cooking equipment had been installed. The huge stove, big enough to use in a restaurant kitchen, was never used. All the food was carried in from outside cooking areas. I learned that the less elegant buildings, that were built against the inside of the walls, were used for cooking, laundry, and repairs. In addition, buildings along the inside walls held apartments or living quarters for the hoards of servants and slaves that did the work of keeping the place running smoothly.

The departing nurse, Kelly had told me I could call anywhere in the world on the phones. The English nurses chatted daily with their friends in the UK, anytime they chose. At that time, I didn't know about the international country codes, had never heard of them. I couldn't make the connections, try as I might.

The next day began as usual and, later in the morning, the British nurse, Liz arrived. She was a tall, slim, and lovely dark-haired girl, back from her leave home. She appeared to be very tired. I suggested she get some rest. She went to their nurses' quarters to sleep.

When Liz returned to care for the princess, she told me about their personal lives, living in and about the palace. They were allowed some activities outside the palace such as shopping. If they were invited, they were also permitted to attend a few parties around Riyadh.

They often roller skated about the grounds on the sidewalks. She laughed as she told me, "They love to watch us, especially when we fall down. They get a big kick out of that."

Those girls felt more isolation from their countrymen more than we did, as there were just the few of them. After a time it became extremely important for all of us to get out of the kingdom and go on holiday. It is necessary, mentally, if only to get your head on straight again. How can I explain that? I don't think it's possible to explain that feeling to someone who has only known a complete sense of personal freedom.

Liz escorted me to the nurses' apartment. I found it serviceable, but nothing elegant. I showered, read a book, napped, and answered the door when they brought me a tray of food. This time the tray was enameled, with crockery dishes, but the food was of the same high quality as in the princess's chambers.

The tall young Arab man who brought it asked, "*Liz hina?*" Is Liz here?

In my hackneyed Arabic, I told him she was with the *Emira,* the princess. That he found the dark-eyed, dark-haired, young British nurse of interest was a given. He'd obviously missed the sight of her during her holiday.

The next day, after the re-appearance of the nurse, Liz, I was given a fat envelope by the princess's mother and, without looking inside, put it in my suitcase. Later, as I heaved a sigh of relief, the same doctor drove me home.

As I walked to my unit, I heard someone make a remark about visiting a palace to take care of a prince in every way. There would always be gossip. It wasn't pleasant, and there was no defense against something like that as far as I knew.

When I reached my quarters, I tossed the envelope on the table. "Tessa, look in there—see what's in it. The princess's mother handed it to me with a nod of thanks before I left."

Tessa was home because she had contracted chicken pox from a young Saudi patient, four-year-old Abdulraman. She resembled a picture-perfect example of chicken pox patients I'd seen as a child in a book of communicable diseases.

She picked it up, hefted it, and we opened it together. It contained a thick sheaf of 100 *Riyal* bills. There were thirty of them in all. It came to nearly eight hundred American dollars. Not bad for twenty seven hours at a palace, and a totally unexpected look into one small part of the intimate lives of Saudi women.

Royal or not, I had the impression that the women of this country lived a boring life of seclusion, gossip, shopping, and bearing children. Each day followed the same pattern as the day before, with occasional outings to visit other women. If married, they still spent most of their time in the company of other females with one-upmanship the prime mover in their relationships.

Chapter 8

Another Compound

Invited to another party, Tessa and I climbed aboard a bus along with several others on our way to yet another unknown location. Arriving in darkness, it seemed eerily quiet for a party, or was it really a party? We heard nothing and saw nothing inside the high eight foot iron walls. Entering the house, still nothing, but ascending the marble stairs toward the third floor, I had the feeling the roof was undulating up and down with the intensity of the blaring music. The Brits like good, solid music with a strong beat. We heard it pounding and it threw us into party mode even before we reached the third floor.

Inside the door, a British nurse we knew, Pam, quickly introduced us to some of the party goers milling around. They were mostly guys, of course. Pam also introduced us to a particular couple of men she thought we would enjoy knowing. We danced a few times with them—me with Dan, and Tessa with Brice. That I had met a very special guy from London had yet to dawn on me.

The alcohol flowed freely, consisting of the usual homemade creations. These Brits were especially adept at brewing a pale beer which they proudly served. They did a good job on that, actually. Dan made sure I had food and beverages but I noticed his solicitous treatment of everyone else as well.

The pool table had been pushed aside, covered with a sheet, and laid out with tons of good looking food. They had a Thai cook who must have been a genius of sorts. They served tiny chicken legs, actually the big part of a wing, in a delicious sauce. There was shrimp in a sauce, bright vegetables, dumplings, fruits of many kinds, tiny beef ribs, and vegetables fixed in finger-food style. All in all, it was a great and delicious repast set out for us.

This compound held electrical workers who did electrical contracting for certain buildings. These instillations were all done in British style 220 electricity, since whoever built the building, put in the electricity the same as in their home country. A hodgepodge really, but that was the way it was at the time. One building had the wiring for 110, the next one 220. Saudi Arabians must have needed a lot of converters for the appliances they used.

We had a great evening and met wonderful people. For me I think I soon realized I had met one of the nicest men I've ever known, Dan. Tessa made a date with her Brice, but I hadn't made any arrangements. After we went home, and for several weeks thereafter, the memory lingered on. I kept remembering how generously Dan took care of the guests that night, how he kept everyone eating, dancing, and enjoying themselves. Most of all, he was closer to my age and not married. Tall, broad shouldered, and handsome with his thick mop of silver streaked hair, he looked very fine to me.

Several weeks later, we went to AMA again. I sought him with my eyes. He was there and looked for me as well. After that we spent more time together. I found myself suffering a twinge of jealousy when Pam, fancying herself a very fine mover and shaker, took him out on the dance floor. Tessa, busy with Brice, spent long hours in his company as well. Dan asked me out and we dated often after that, and a happy time it became for we two.

Dan ran a crew of Thai electricians who were busy wiring a palace in Riyadh. I saw him stand before his men, speaking in their tongue, to issue his orders and answer their concerns. He cared enough about them to learn their language and speak to them as equals. I have to say I was very impressed by that, as well as what fun he was to be with.

He hailed from London and used the local language as well. Passing a truck, he called it a Lorry. A semi rig, he referred to as an articulated lorry, and we stopped for petrol instead of gasoline. Though completely natural on his part, I found it charming.

Riyadh had a very fine Thai restaurant, with a side room for families to dine, and Dan introduced me to Thai food. My first taste of the fiery shrimp soup, *tam yum* shrimp, nearly took my breath away, but I loved it. We ate there very often and always ordered it.

We also ate at The Carvery where they served camel meat. This restaurant rated a bit above many Riyadh eating places. A few times we worried about being caught by the *Matawas*, the religious police. For some reason, they seemed to hang about that place. When we saw them, we quietly faded away to our cars after we finished eating. Seeing them caused our innate paranoia to spring forth.

Dan took me to a palace they were wiring. It belonged to a Royal prince who had it built for his American bride. It had an indoor and outdoor swimming pool, bowling alleys, putting greens, and it sat three stories high, with any number of wonderful, gold-encrusted, furnished rooms. To me, knowing more about the Kingdom these days, I saw it only as a lovely, gilded cage.

Knowing that her husband held her passport, and her life in his hands, took the wonder out of that lovely palace. She could not go to an embassy or even go shopping without his permission. I couldn't imagine how any American woman could place herself in that situation. Possibly she didn't know what could happen to her in marrying a man from the Kingdom. No woman is really free when her husband holds the power of life or death over her.

No law protects her. He *is* the law over her. If her husband decides she is no longer what he wants, he may divorce her and any children they have will remain with him. She cannot change that or challenge it. Many American women are currently trying to get custody of children born during their marriage to Saudi men. I haven't heard of many successes, if any. Aside from those dark thoughts, we had a wonderful day.

Seeing that gilded palace made me remember a woman we had once seen on the streets of Riyadh. We believed her to be an American and since she was alone at that moment, we decided to speak with her. Judy and I approached her and asked where she came from. Never in our lives had we seen such fear in a woman's eyes.

She mumbled a few words in English while glancing nervously about and we instantly knew she feared for her life, should she displease her husband. We quickly left her, lest she be accused of betraying whoever he was. But we never forgot that experience. It haunts us to this day. What a happy girl she must have been in marrying a handsome man from another country. Could he have been a foreign student studying in The States perhaps? She couldn't possibly have imagined the terrible fate that lay before her. Whoever could?

Dan and I were often invited out as a couple and I still have one of the invitations to read and remember. On one occasion, Tessa and I decided to make dinner for Dan and Andrew, a big Scotsman she knew. Andrew lived in a small mobile home at the edge of a dry desert wash, or waterway. We planned on making Mexican food for the guys and they were more than ready for the fun of having us cook for them, as well as enjoying our companionship.

We toiled away and the men, eager as little boys, kept checking on our progress. In making tea for them we were careful not to make it too strong. When they both proclaimed it tasted like gnat's piss, we learned we hadn't let it brew long enough. Aside from the gnat's piss, we had a wonderful evening, one remembered fondly, if not passionately.

A few weeks later, a big storm came up and the water course beside Andrew's mobile became flooded. Awakened from a sound sleep, he opened his door to find the water so high it had begun to toss his home about in the flooded stream bed. He leaped out in time to save his life, but hours later the authorities found a big, naked Scotsman clinging to a small tree alongside the roaring stream. He'd lost all his personal belongings and barely escaped with his life.

Andrew was able to laugh about it but the experience changed the man in some way. He left off seeing most of his closest friends and broke up with any women he dated as well. We never understood what that was all about.

Dan took me to visit Dir'iyah, a crumbling mud village the Turks had destroyed many years ago. It had once been a bustling city and lay just outside Riyadh. Many old date palms still grew there, and many people, Saudi and otherwise, came to walk the byways and imagine the lives once lived there. Did we find secret rooms where they hid away the females? We thought so, seeing old panels of thin sticks used to screen someone from view, but how could we be sure? The fun lay in using our imagination about lives lived so long ago. Mostly, I remember his big body walking along beside me in fine companionship.

The time came when Dan got orders to return to London. This was a sorry day for both of us. I became one of the sorrowing ladies left behind in Riyadh, like so many others I had seen.

Chapter 9

The Princess

J udy, we have a Saudi princess who is here from the United States, and she is very ill. You will sit with her today." With that, the charge nurse, Chang, assigned Judy to a long and touching relationship with a most unfortunate Saudi woman. Princess or not, being a woman of the Kingdom of Saudi Arabia has its hazards as we were to learn intimately.

Entering the room, Judy found a sleeping woman in her thirties occasionally moaning and writhing in her bed in confusion. Her linens were mussed and twisted due to her thrashing about in a confused state. The report stated that the woman was in a state of drugged euphoria.

During the months Judy "minded the princess," a strange and tragic tale emerged. Princess, as she is named here, was born to a ruling king of Saudi Arabia, King Saud. She was one of his 110 or more, children. Her mother, a princess of Syria, was one of the four wives allowed (at a time) under the teachings of the Holy Koran.

Her father, who soon earned the title of The Wastrel King, had in time, been deposed by his brother Faisal. During her father's reign, at his discretion and choice, Princess, aged eleven, had been given in marriage. She bore the man a son, who was twelve years her junior.

Her father, King Saud, spent money wildly. He denied himself, his friends, and family, nothing. Upon his deposal, the family fled to Greece under the protection of King Constantine who gave them asylum. The now ex-king, Saud, Princess's mother, Princess, and a sister were together there. The whereabouts of her son remained unknown to her. Children usually remain with the father when couples separate, no matter if they are of royal birth or not. Perhaps her mother's royal status made a difference that enabled the daughters to remain with the mother.

During her time in Greece, her father, ex-king Saud, was murdered. The mother took her daughters and fled to Syria under the protection of the president of that country—he being their grandfather. After a few years, the girls attended school in France. During that time, they wrote a book about their troubles in the Saudi Kingdom that the world might know what had happened to their family, in particular, their father, the ex-king.

This book detailed corruption within the royal family and the machinations involved in the deposing of their father. The book, written in the French language, was first published in France. The king of Saudi Arabia, Faisal, discovered the book and by edict, had it removed from publication and every edition destroyed. After this, the sisters fled to England where they believed they were safe.

In England, Princess's sister was eventually murdered, shot to death in London on a Christmas Day. Princess then fled to America, finally buying a home in Malibu, California where she set up a household and attracted a large circle of friends. She tended to drink to excess and use drugs, perhaps trying to forget the tragedies of her younger life.

During her years of living freely in the confines of the United States, she frequently made derogatory remarks against the ruling family of Saudi Arabia. She daily cursed the Saudi King and it was not appreciated by the current monarch, Fahd. This fact finally led to her being drugged during a routine clinic visit, taken aboard a private plane, and flown away from freedom, into captivity, at the command of an angry king.

Previously arranged with a traitorous doctor and his nurse wife, Princess was kept drugged during flights aboard a small private plane that eventually reached Riyadh. Princess told Judy she believed they were paid about one million dollars for their part in her abduction.

According to hospital scuttlebutt, both the doctor and his wife were held in Saudi Arabia for a time before being allowed to leave the kingdom. It's too bad those two weren't given a pretty little palace in which to spend the rest of their lives. (This became the fate of Princess.)

During the many months of "minding the princess," the lady confided these things to her caregivers. She called her friends in Malibu daily, having long, unhappy, conversations with them. Her longing for the freedom of America became heartbreakingly evident. Her caregivers, or watch dogs, as the case may be, grew close to Princess in her suffering. She preferred American nurses to any other and requested them always.

The king frequently came to the hospital to visit his sick brother, who had medical problems during that time. He did not come to see Princess. Extremely fearful of him during those visits, Princess preferred to stay hidden in her room, though she would on occasion walk in the hall, but only near the security of her room. She chatted with her caregivers and looked out the windows during those times the king might be near.

Escape was never an option for Princess. She had no passport or support system for anything like that. For a royal-born personage such as she, escape could mean living in lowered circumstances. It seemed unlikely she would be able to give up the trappings of royalty and the comforts and privileges of wealth. Her royal upbringing evidently made it impossible for her to consider living like a refugee.

Her appearance and health improved steadily during her stay at King Faisal Specialist Hospital. She watched endless movies, preferring American and French films. She often sent her chauffeur out for special foods for herself and her sitters to enjoy. Only occasionally did she watch Arabic language films.

Frequently, at the mention of the king, she was to utter her most fervent statement regarding him, "F----the king!" Hurt and anguished at her situation, she expressed her distress in American fashion. Statements of this sort could not possibly have helped her situation, but it never hampered her verbal hatred of the king.

During the long months of her hospital incarceration, the king had a lovely little palace built for her. It had seven bathrooms, with Jacuzzis, and was filled with the finest marble, gold fixtures, and luxurious furnishings.

The furnishings, very expensive and ornate, included a huge dining table that boasted a large silver domed tray atop the glossy surface. Green-veined marble lined the baths, huge plushy couches graced the living room, and even her doors were carved most magnificently and bore the finest of hardware.

Maids and a chauffeur were supplied. After she was moved there, she knew the servants reported her every movement to the king. She was a bird in a lovely, gilded cage. Her situation was unthinkable and extremely sad to free thinking and moving Americans who visited her upon occasion.

Against all advice from her American friends, she refused the veil and wore jeans beneath the *abaya* on her shopping trips to purchase a suitable garment to wear during her requested audience before the king, her uncle. Her plea during her appearance before him was that she be allowed to return to the freedoms of America. It was not granted.

Dressing improperly didn't help her cause, since that rebellion was seen as an act of defiance by the king. Bad-mouthing the king was the primary cause of her incarceration in the first place. Being royal herself, perhaps she felt she could do as she pleased without consequence. But in the end, she was only a Saudi female, and she couldn't.

Her American friends continually tried to advise her against these acts of defiance, but without success. Only fear of death caused her to comply with female Saudi custom. She did not pray, that we were aware of, and cursed the King with nearly every breath.

At last report she remains in Riyadh, ensconced in her palatial prison.

Chapter 10

Party at Wackenhut

On a rainy day in Riyadh, Judy learned about an unusual party at Wackenhut. Her friend George, a handsome Brit, a man with severe character flaws (she learned later), had informed her about the party. He worked at this facility and suggested we all go. He never told us it was "fancy dress" or better described as partially "fancy undress."

Before we were ready to go to the event, George tried to scratch the idea. But things had gotten too far along for that and, later, we learned why.

That night Riyadh was blasted with a flooding rainstorm, which made our getting to the party hazardous. Should we have an accident, our presence in a car with a male who was not a close relative could cause our ouster from the Kingdom. Constantly guilty of this, we were never caught.

Later we learned that the class system in England is alive and well. George had one h---- of a time getting into the party because his job and social status didn't qualify him for entrance to the festivities. Why they did let him in remains a mystery. Maybe it was because he was accompanied by two American ladies. Women were a high priority at any party.

Entering the ballroom, or what purported to be one, we discovered we were supposed to remove our trousers and just wear whatever we had on beneath. This American flatly refused and so did Judy. We condescended to roll our jeans up a roll or two, but no more than that. With that done we joined the party which included lots of dancing, food, and the usual alcoholic brews so freely offered.

Of interest was the staid English's slightly upper crust idea of "fancy dress." One noble gentleman wore a lovely tuxedo sans the pants, socks with garters attached to hairy English legs. His long feet were shod with fancy, shiny oxfords with the backs missing.

We saw any number of those backless shoes downtown in the store windows, since these are Saudi style dress shoes. Why were they made this way? Maybe because they were easy to slip into? Probably, or they just like to differ from the Westerner. With these shoes, they didn't have to bend over and tie laces. Thus he could save his energy for lengthy discourses over their strong bitter coffee, which seemed to be a Saudi pastime.

The man was a good dancer and tried to talk to me, though little conversation could be heard over the loud, crashing music. Upper crust or not, they liked their music loud. I felt very uncomfortable dancing with a partially clad man. I don't remember his face, only his clothes and stuffy mien.

Outside we saw the wistful faces of George's co-workers who were not allowed in to enjoy the party. We felt badly for those left out, but that feeling wasn't shared by the higher-classed British revelers inside.

We watched some of the women, much better pre-pared for this bash, wearing skimpy underwear-type clothing which emphasized their particular assets. We didn't feel bad about how we dressed. We had a good time and left for our compound in time to beat the cur-few.

Aside from the party business, George shook his head in disbelief as he regaled us with a tale of fighting fire in Riyadh. Part of his duties included manning the fire truck when needed. One night a raging fire occurred in downtown Riyadh. They were asked to respond and did so.

When they reached the scene, one fire truck, manned by Saudis, was there fighting the fire. They stopped work on the fire when another fire truck, manned by Saudis pulled up. All fire-fighting stopped until greetings were properly done. The kissing and *wa salaam alaykums* and *wa alaykum as salaams* were done with each truck's members. After the greetings, they commenced to spray water on the building, now nearly consumed by the roaring flames.

They sprayed for a short time until they decided it was the will of Allah that the fire would consume the building. They packed up their equipment and left the scene. The Wackenhut men were left on their own, shaking their heads at the difference in thought and ideas between their two countries.

Chapter 11

Africa

My third year, and Judy's second, became the year everyone went to Africa on Safari. We listened repeatedly to tales of exotic balloon safaris over the Maasai Mara, looking down upon the beautiful creatures that live in Africa, and the conducted tours of Abercrombie and Kent. Everyone had wonderful pictures and shared them eagerly. Seeing and hearing these things created flurries of excitement, especially for Judy and me.

One can stand only so much enticement. In my entire life, the thought of going on safari in Africa had never entered my mind as a possibility, except in day dreams after watching an old Tarzan movie. Things like that only happen in travelogues or jungle movies. However, under the influence of such wonderful tales, Judy and I decided to go.

We planned our trip within our limited experience, secure in the knowledge we would be in good company with Judy's friend, George. He was now living in England, but would join us in Nairobi. Many adventures are caused by stupidity and poor planning, a lesson we tended to learn more than once.

Instead of the nice routine flight to Nairobi from Riyadh on Saudia, an airline we were very familiar with, we chose to fly Kenya Airways to save a day. After arriving in Jedda, the jumping off place for flights to everywhere, it was all downhill from there.

We sat patiently waiting for our flight, surrounded by tall men with glossy-black faces, wearing white turban-topped head wear or a fez-like hat. The women were dressed in soft tones of orange and/or tan, with touches of black, which were so common among Africans.

Many of the Africans had young children with them, but I don't recall any sounds of crying or misbehaving while we awaited our flight. Most of their baggage consisted of large, cloth-wrapped bundles, or the occasional huge suitcase proudly proclaiming "*Happy journey*" on the side. They sat about on the floor, calmly awaiting the short hop to Khartoum.

The Sudanese are generally very tall, and the men wrap long white strips of cloth around their heads creating an even taller look. I have said numerous times that "Every man is a king in the Sudan because of that regal-appearing headdress."

The departure board said 04:30. As time passed it was after 06:30 and the board still proclaimed 04:30, and said: On time. Though we were stressed by the discrepancy, the Sudanese patiently waited. We finally boarded and quickly realized we were the only whites on the flight. It gives one pause after always being in the majority. At no time did we feel uncomfortable, and this was a flight to Africa, after all.

Treated to scramble seating, we made our way to the back row. I took the window seat, and Judy, the aisle. The plane was packed. A very tall gentleman asked either of us to move to accommodate him, but we wouldn't change our seats.

Without argument, he heaved a sigh, hiked up his long white dress, stepped over Judy and took his seat in the center. He had a box of luggage that his feet rested on, his long knees reaching skyward. We departed for Khartoum, the Sudan's major city. It was dawn when we passed over the Red Sea and again, I felt a thrill seeing a sight I had only read about.

Looking out the window held my attention, but Judy sitting in the aisle seat, felt nauseous. We rode with a plane-load of people so seemingly different from us. Perhaps the gentle, fuggy odor of semi-washed bodies among those who rarely, if ever used deodorant, had affected her.

Later in the flight, our seat-mate whipped out a razor blade, which left me feeling edgy and Judy ever more nauseous. He commenced shaving off the grey powder that had at one time been his fingernails. As the grayish shavings drifted downward, he asked me in Arabic what he should do about the condition of his nails. Only one nail had a semblance of normalcy.

The national language of Sudan is Arabic, so we could converse, though barely. In my hackneyed Arabic I recommended he see a doctor. I realized afterward, he'd probably never seen a doctor in his entire life. I didn't know the word for vinegar, or fungus, which might have helped.

Judy, seeing the nail shaving, and razor blade, reached for the nearest barf bag but found it had already been used. Reaching across the aisle, she found that one filled as well. We'll never know on what flight it had been used. And shortly thereafter, they served lunch.

I don't recall what was served, but the bread lingers in my mind as about the best bread I've ever eaten. Ethnic breads are usually delicious, but this was more so. Judy found everything disgusting, including me. Being nauseous, she ate little.

Later our seat-mate broke into a sweat, groaned, and murmured softly, "Malaria," while mopping his brow.

This added one more treasure to our African misadventure.

As we circled Khartoum in preparation to land, below us we saw the conjoining of the Blue Nile and the White Nile. These rivers combine to become The Nile which flows down through Egypt. It's wonderfully exciting to see something you've only heard about, or read about. Thanks to the author, Wilbur Smith, a South African who wrote many books about Africa, and Egypt as well, occasionally mentioning the origins of the Nile River, we knew about it. And there it was below us.

Landing, we saw a sight that brought tears to our eyes. Before us, in all its glory to semi-homesick Americans, there sat a presidential Boeing 747 airplane with the United States of America emblazoned across it.

Later, we found out it was the Vice President, George H. W. Bush. Why he was there, we never knew for certain, but someone said he visited the Sudanese Government to warn them we would be bombing Muammar Qaddafi of Libya in the near future. That did happen a few months later. All the Arab governments had been informed and gave tacit agreement, but took no part in the assault.

Later on, because this bombing had taken place, Judy and I cancelled a scheduled trip to Egypt, though several Egyptian girls told us they were glad about the bombing. They said the Libyan government often hired Egyptian workers to come to Libya for employment. Though they were fed and housed, when it came time to pay the wages, they were kicked out of the country with no transportation home and no payment for their services. This treatment left strong resentment among the Egyptian populace. Thus they bore only fear and distrust of the Libyans.

In Khartoum, we found their airport system completely confusing, but one has to learn to trust in a situation like that. We were worried about our luggage, and an official of the airport took us where it could be seen. It was within a huge pile of luggage on a wheeled cart, and we caught a glimpse of ours, only to see it disappear again. We gave away a few perfume samples in thanks for their help. Those were well received. We finally quit worrying about the luggage. It solved nothing.

Eventually, we ended up waiting for the flight to Nairobi in a small, airless, white-washed room. The slight odor of toilet, semi-washed bodies, and the buzzing of numerous flies assaulted our senses. Waiting, we chatted with some of the passengers around us. One man attempted to set us up with a relative in Mombasa, since we had mentioned we were going there. He said he knew a nice place this person had for rent. We thanked him, saying we'd made our reservations.

We mentioned that the plane was two hours late. One soft-spoken gentleman offered his timely comment: "Sometimes, they two hours late, sometimes…they two days late."

Everyone else remained calm, but we looked at each other with rising panic at that news. We didn't know if the Sudanese were friendly to stranded American females.

Eventually, we took off for Nairobi. Reaching our highest altitude, the pilot announced. "We won't be landing at Juba, due to the sand storm." Outside our plane windows, reddish dust was thick in the air making it easy to believe the stories of the Sahara advancing downward over Africa, replacing green jungle with arid red sands. There it was, in a roiling, reddish dust cloud outside our plane!

We looked at each other and said, "Juba?" Unaware that it was a stop on the itinerary, we felt relieved we weren't going there.

Landing at Nairobi, we were met by our British friend, George. How he knew to meet us, after my giving him all the wrong flight numbers, we'll never know. But in spite of all the mix-ups, we were glad to see someone we knew. At the Stanley Hotel we showered, relaxed, and felt at ease—we'd made it, after all.

Nairobi is big and busy, with lots of traffic, and people of all colors, though primarily black. We walked the streets, shopped for safari clothes, and found they are manufactured by the Kenyans. The shirt bodies are made slim with longer sleeves befitting the African body style. They were of soft, printed cotton and generally of muted animal prints, just fine for safari wear. At that, they were no doubt made for tourist wear, even with the sleeves three inches too long.

The people of Kenya make as many of their own products as possible. We saw matchbook covers, soap products, food stuffs, facial tissues, and nearly everything used, carried the "Made in Kenya" label. It created jobs, helped the balance of payments, and then there was the thriving tourist business. That created more jobs than any other business as far as we knew.

Handmade crafts were displayed on the sidewalks. Native carvings, inventive and very artistic, were a treasure and we loaded up. Everyone we met was friendly, although we were told not to go very far from the hotel after dark. One man from Uganda followed us, shaking his fist at George, calling him nasty names and accusing us of racism.

He yelled at George, "You hate us, you call us monkeys!" We hurried away from him, since an altercation would only have worsened the situation.

Already warned not to rent a car in Kenya, or to trust their maps, we were foolish for certain. After all, we had a man traveling with us and that became the deciding factor—poor George.

Renting a car, we drove out of Nairobi to the Kenya National Game Preserve. Warned to stay inside our car, we followed this good advice which became especially important when we met a family of baboons. The biggest male jumped onto the hood of our car and tried to get his hands inside. We managed to roll our windows up just in time. He satisfied himself by snarling, showing his ugly yellowed teeth, and screaming his displeasure at our presence. That experience made us realize we never wanted to meet baboons in an unprotected situation.

We saw lions, zebra, giraffes, and huge Cape Buffalos with white egrets clustered about them, busily picking at fleas and scratching in the manure so plentiful from these cattle-like creatures. Cattle they may appear to be, but we learned that they kill more unsuspecting tourists and natives than any other creature on the African plains.

A river had many hippos in and around it, and those are very deadly to tourists as well. We'd already learned to avoid them and watched the rounded mounds of them, spending their day suspended in the slightly muddy river, from a safe distance.

We chased a few ostriches with the car to watch them run away on their big blue or pink legs. It would have been nice to see one of their nests with those huge eggs, but we didn't. They are unbelievably huge birds, especially outlined against a setting sun.

Giraffes graze on the high branches of fever or acacia trees, and we saw a large herd of them having dinner. They had no fear of us and this made for a great photo-op. They looked rather majestic against the lacy green trees.

Later in a city animal park we saw black and green mambas, about the most deadly snakes on earth. That they were behind glass made us feel better. They aren't large snakes but both the black and green ones are incredibly poisonous.

The biggest African elephant ever caught had been preserved for all to see. The monster-sized elephant, though stuffed, was massive and very exciting.

Leaving Nairobi, we drove in our rented car through Thicka, which brought to mind the TV series, *The Flame Trees of Thicka.* There is something deeply satisfying to see a place only heard of from a TV program. It was a rather dry, dusty plain. We saw many trees covered with thick masses of flame-colored flowers. The area was totally wonderful, and we drove through those trees for many miles.

On the way to the Mount Kenya Safari Club we saw people clustered about the highway. In the middle of the road lay the still form of a woman who had been struck dead by a car. She wore the orange-brown printed wrap of so many women in Africa.

We made it to Mount Kenya Safari Club, a very posh resort co-owned by Adnan Kashoggi, William Holden, and Stephanie Powers. We stayed in the personal cabin of William Holden and Stephanie Powers. It was hardly a cabin, with a shower as big as full bathroom, a fireplace, and three bedrooms. Actually, it had everything. It was beautiful.

Dinner is included with African accommodations. We dressed nicely for it, but George had no dinner jacket and had to wait until they brought one for him so he would be presentable. The full-course dinner of roast beef, chicken, or another meat, with an assortment of vegetables was elegantly served by dark-skinned waiters. Included were drinks and assorted desserts.

It was truly a luxury stay. This was a magnificent place, straddling the equator, with Mount Kenya, snow-capped and floating on the horizon in a hazy mist. The native dancers and colorful wild birds all about the place only added to its charm. Wild animals roamed freely and without fear in this sanctuary. The main purpose of the resort was a haven for the wild beasts of Africa. Of course, lions and elephants were missing, or we didn't see any. They keep the elephants out of the path of humans as much as possible.

My one regret is that I forgot to see how the water ran when I flushed the toilet. It is clock-wise in the Northern Hemisphere and counter clock-wise in the Southern, but what about right on the equator? I'll have to go there again to check that out.

All good things must come to an end. We left this island of ultimate luxury and followed the map to find the Tree Tops Jungle lodge. We traveled to the Outspan Hotel in Nyeri. Outspan is a term generally meaning unhooking the oxen for the night when you are on a trek. This term came from the Boer settlers who came to Africa in the 1700s. England later tried to boot them out without success, hence the Boer Wars.

From there we were driven to Tree Tops Jungle Lodge via a huge Land Rover. It wasn't all up in the trees as in its infancy, because when Jomo Kenyatta held power in Kenya he burned it down. It was rebuilt, using several huge trees and many tall posts. It is very grand and meets the purpose intended. From the walkways high above the jungle floor, we could watch exotic African animals in safety. It contained wide verandas to walk upon, the better for viewing.

The Jungle Lodge where Princess Elizabeth became queen in 1952 does not exist, except in memory. It is said she walked unafraid to the ladder with a few wild African elephants in close attendance. She had to have been a very brave woman or felt her royal status would protect her.

We found ourselves high above the jungle floor in a comfortable and safe environment. The rambling, two-story structure contained gift shops, sleeping rooms, and dining facilities. Looking over the edges of the verandas, we searched the area for elephants. We saw more wart hogs rooting about on their knees than anything else. We also saw gazelles, buffalo, water bucks, baboons, and many species of birds. They grazed unafraid, on patches of dry looking grass below us, and had no fear of each other as they came to drink at the large water hole that attracted them.

After enjoying a very fine dinner, we watched the darkness descend over the jungle and chatted with several other tourists before seeking our beds. After an early breakfast the next morning, they returned us to the Outspan Hotel where we continued on our way toward Lake Victoria.

That journey took us over the Mau Escarpment filled with tea plantations. We tried to enter one of the plantations just to see how they dried the tea, but found they were under guard and visitors were not allowed. No one explained the reason for their paranoia. A tour guide would have been great about then.

We came to the Sunset Hotel in Kisumu at the edge of Lake Victoria. This lake is so huge it has gigantic waves when the wind comes up. Large steamers provide transportation across the lake as well. It also supports a very profitable fishing industry. The refrigeration wasn't working so our complexions enjoyed a nice steam treatment.

We decided to go into town and exchange a few traveler's checks. We wore shorts thinking it proper attire. Wrong! Imagine feeling immodestly dressed in a small African city. We did and decided to shop in a local store. It had no air conditioning, and was a bit stuffy inside. We found suitable cotton skirts and tops to match, (all Kenyan made), and put them on.

We drove around a few unpaved streets and, when we stopped, African children did their best to climb into our car. We asked them what they wanted. One little girl said with her British sort of accent, "We wish to enter."

As she stepped into our car, she had no worries about abduction or molestation. She was in total innocence of such things.

We found them very charming and it helped us to understand the un-worldliness of the African in his/her own setting. We saw this many times on our tour of this marvelous continent.

Changing money in a small African town is an experience in its self. They seated us and took a look at a $100.00 Traveler's check. Our clerk went to check with his manager. Two other men put their heads together and finally, George's British traveler's check was taken and papers were painstakingly made out then pinned at the corner with a straight pin, instead of being stapled together. After much fuss and feathers, we each went through the same process. After nearly two hours, we departed the bank with our Kenyan pounds.

As we were driving back to Nairobi, we stopped at Lake Nukuru National Park. In travel documentaries they show clouds of pink flamingos flying up and whirling over the huge shallow lake and that is exactly what we saw as well. Magical to the eyes, there were millions of these delicate, thin legged birds clothed with many shades of pink plumage. Other animals frequent that area but we saw nothing overly exciting for the moment.

On our way again, we stopped along the road and bought things. Many young natives we met gave us their addresses in hopes of hearing from us later. I bought a beautiful white sheep-skin, never imagining it would become a gift of gratitude later on.

In Nairobi again, we stayed at a hotel named 680. It wasn't great at all! But in the morning we were on our way to Amboseli National Park at the foot of Mount Kilimanjaro. We had reservations at the Serena Lodge. Pricey, but it included tours, out to see the animals, and all of our meals.

Later on, we got off the proper road by following a very small and inadequate map, and I took personal responsibility for that dreadful error. Maps in Arizona were reliable, but maps in Africa were not. Also, unfortunately, we began our off-road adventure with one fourth of a tank of gas. As an Arizonian I wouldn't have begun anything along wilderness lines without a full tank, but George was from England where distances are small. Perhaps a full gas tank didn't seem so important to him or maybe he never checked on it. I know I didn't.

Leaving a broad, well-traveled, gravel road, we turned onto a much narrower one. As it meandered along, we saw zebra, giraffe, gazelles, and multitudes of birds. Maasai tribal people, mostly the younger ones, grazed cattle in many areas. In time, we came to a store and George went in to ask directions.

When he came out his face was pale and he was very eager to get away from the place. "They're all Maasai natives in there and some of the women weren't wearing much on top except ornaments and beads." This seemed like a very good place to leave behind. We eagerly drove on, crossing a wide sandy waterway, dry at the moment.

"They indicated we should go this way," George said. He pointed toward the East where the faint outlines of Mt. Kilimanjaro lay against the skyline.

Our tank had reached the critically low level by now, but maybe we could make it. The track became more of a narrow, bushy, trail. We kept on until George declared in a definite tone, "We must head back to the store. We have to."

After a few minutes of heading toward the store, our car coughed and died. We were out of gas. We had no choice but to walk back toward a store that had seemed so frightening earlier.

George held firm, saying, "We have to walk back to that store." We made no attempt to argue the point. That forbidding place now seemed a haven of safety since we no longer had the car's metal body for shelter. Looking back, we realized George had been as frightened as we were.

We took what water we had, our colorfully woven Kenya bags, and two beach towels and set out. It may have been the middle of the afternoon, but the sun was heading down and we were out in the open. Walking along the track, we looked for possible trees we might climb if threatened by wild animals.

"Look at those hideous thorns!" I cried, taking a closer look at an Acacia tree. "How could you climb one of those if a lion comes?"

African trees may be lovely to look at but to climb one would strip the flesh off arms and legs. They all bore large sharp thorns. The fever or Acacia trees are the same. It was true that giraffes eat the fine fern-like leaves from around the thorns, but the trunks were covered with the inhospitable thorns about one inch in diameter at their base and protruding into a deadly sharp point at their outer end. Then, we noticed that the other trees were about as friendly.

Judy became tired, moved ever slower, and limped.

"Judy," I said. "I don't want to be out here after dark."

Hearing that, she picked up the pace for a while, but soon lagged behind again. Seeing giraffes nipping at the tops of fever trees and zebras running wild made us wonder if lions could be far behind. We become increasingly uneasy. We saw no other humans and the sun sank ever lower.

Struggling to make a bit of time, nagging at my friend as much as I dared, we moved along. I said too many times, "Judy, keep moving. I don't want to be out here after dark."

She finally said, "Go on, leave me here to die. I can't walk any faster."

We kept on. Nearing dusk, George spotted three native men attending a campfire. When he approached them, he saw the men were cooking an animal head covered with flies. We watched him chatting or gesturing with those men.

George came back to us, because we had lagged behind, to tell us. "They're dead friendly, Jude." He took her arm for support.

We approached the men and the tallest one, who had friendly appearing features, made a gesture of hospitality to us. He put his hands together and lay them beside his face, indicating we could sleep in their village for the night. We decided to follow these men. We learned later that men cannot cook meat in front of women, so that must be the reason they were out there. How much meat could you get off a fly-covered animal head anyway?

Were we afraid? At that time we only remembered that they were human beings and looked extremely good to us in our situation. We knew nothing of these people at the time. They were a part of the proud Maasai tribe. We learned much more about them after the fact, but at the time, they were just people and looked mighty good to us.

Approaching the village, we saw it was completely encompassed by a good sized rounded fence, consisting of thorn bushes made into a thick, wide roll that went all the way around the cluster of huts. Just outside the village, a native woman, wearing only wide beaded rings around her neck, and nothing else on top, gave us a very unfriendly look. She carried a naked child of several months on her hip. Though his eyes and nose were clogged with flies, he looked fat and healthy.

We entered through the opening in the thorn fence and saw several men standing around, taking us in. No one spoke our language, so explanations were not an option. One smaller man excitedly urged us to come into a hut. George and I went in first with Judy following. Their huts are constructed of mud and cow dung plastered onto wooden frameworks. The odor was one of mustiness. It was exceptionally dim inside as we edged into the narrow entryway along one side. It opened out into what appeared to be two rooms divided a bit by a hanging cloth. This wasn't our idea of a room at the Hilton, but we had stopped worrying about being eaten by lions.

When the little man began digging into George's Kenya bag, he became alarmed and said, "Back out of here, we can't stay here. We have to go on to the store."

We edged back out of the hut and sought out our friendly warrior. George indicated to him that we wanted to continue on to the store. We asked the warrior to accompany us. I know how to plead with my hands now.

We left as the moon was on the rise. Judy, ever the social one, walked slowly past the line of warriors and spent time trying to thank them for their hospitality.

George, exasperated, finally spoke up. "Jude, come on!" And we moved out of the compound, heading in exactly the wrong way. Our warrior—named Sweta, we lat-

er learned—laughed and motioned us back to the track
we had been following earlier. From then on, one of the
more charming episodes of our African adventure ensued.

The moon grew ever bigger. We walked along the
track without fear because the Maasai warrior was with
us. George called out, "Come on, Jude!" Then he taught
Sweta to say it.

"Jude!" His white teeth sparkled in the glowing
moonlight as he laughed.

I pointed at the moon and said, "Moon."

Sweta had his word for that, too. He was tall with
handsome features. His hair was short and thick with a
red clay dressing. He wore ear décor imbedded in his
lobes and near the tops of his ears as well. His shoes were
of thick tire tread held together with leather strips fash-
ioned in the manner of his people.

On one shoulder, he wore a drape of orange print
cloth. Now after dark, he wore another strip of cloth on
his other shoulder. He let me heft the ebony wooden staff,
and the spear he carried as well. Both were very heavy
but he looked strong enough to handle them, and did with
ease.

Several times he kept us to the trail and seemed to
enjoy our company. We ambled along under the biggest
moon we'd ever seen, an African moon. George taught
him to say several things, but I didn't understand his
words in return.

Later, he scratched at the front of my skirt in an un-mistakable gesture, but accepted my negative response in good humor. Perhaps I should have been flattered and, in a small way, I was. He also took more than ordinary in-terest in our beach towels and kept fingering them. They were brightly colored, perhaps that was the attraction.

Nearing the store his demeanor changed enough to indicate hesitancy—and even a touch of fear. Nearing the store he finally said a word we knew. He pointed toward the store and said, "Boma!" From what we'd learned around Nairobi, we knew it meant a house or building.

"Hey, Jude," I said. "I speak Swahili now. I know a word."

We crossed again the wide sandy expanse that was a dried water course, adjacent to the store. When we ar-rived there, a man who spoke English and Maasai talked to Sweta and George. When George told them we were afraid of lions attacking, Sweta, as well as the other men, had a good laugh. Maasai men live to kill a lion. It is the mark of their manhood. We knew that now, too.

A group of Maasai had their cattle in the corrals at the store and had camped there for the night as well. Af-ter a time, George gave Sweta some Kenya shillings. The man hugged him and left for his own village.

We were taken to a room at the back of the store. A tin roof sheltered us, and it contained a couch, chair, and a coffee table. It also had electric lights. We had thought we would have to sit on the front porch all night long, fighting off lions, and now we were in a safe place. It was nearly beyond belief to us.

We slowly began to realize the gravity of our situation. No one in the whole of Africa knew where we were, or who we were, for that matter. It was months before all these things really sank in for us. I believe we were numb with not knowing. I know I was.

Just being in this place had all the earmarks of a crazy adventure in itself. After a while, the men of the store brought us food and colas to drink. We enjoyed beans, a piece of potato, and the African style corn bread, which is cornmeal squeezed into a ball and cooked in a broth. I was thrilled to have a chance to eat that because of all the Wilbur Smith books I had read. That style corn bread is often mentioned in his books as a native food.

The adventure deepened when finding out about our hosts. There was John, who spoke some English and ran the store; Williston, who was fluent in English; and Micah, whose tongue had been cut out. He did the cooking.

Williston came from Ongoran-Goran Crater and was at the store with illegal gems to sell to an Italian in Nairobi. We wondered that they would tell us those things. It had all the earmarks of an adventure movie.

Then, luckily for us, the man who serviced the bush stores arrived. He only came there every two weeks. How lucky we were that this was the day! He had a four wheel drive vehicle as well as gasoline. He took George out to get the car.

"If you don't get your car tonight," he explained, "the natives will find it and believe you just left it there. They will think you don't want it anymore, break it open, and take whatever is there."

They returned within an hour and our vehicle was now safe in the yard with all our possessions intact. It sat beside the outdoor toilet we were privileged to use. It was built along Arabian lines having two foot treads and a hole in the middle.

Judy and I also finally realized that our male protector, George, was really terrified of blacks. It slipped out from his demeanor and bits of conversation. He hid it well, but then that man hid a lot of things very well. It came as a surprise to us, and we never had an explanation or an admission regarding his fear of dark-skinned people.

Later, our hosts brought a foam pad and blankets to go with our beach towels. We spent a snug night, while outside, a wild storm raged down on our tin roof. It rapidly filled the once dry riverbed with swiftly running water. Someone, who was very tired at the time, had suggested snuggling down in the sandy riverbed to rest for the night. Thank God that never happened!

No people could have been more hospitable and as long as I live I'll think of Sweta often and bless him. He looked like a good man and he was. Goodness tends to show in a person's face and we never had a qualm about trusting him.

The next morning, before we left them, we prepared gifts for Sweta. For me, I was happy to give him my snowy white fleece. We all wrote on the inside of it, our names and our countries of origin, and our thanks to him. He had given his name and where he could be reached through the men at the store. Though he lived the wild native way, he understood modern ways as well. Sweta Ole Tetile Sankulei Scheme Orkeriai—we thanked you then, we will always thank you…

The man with the petrol gave us enough gasoline, oops…petrol, to get to the highway safely. They served us a breakfast of flat bread and scrambled eggs with coffee. They charged very little for our accommodations and wished us well as we left them.

After our meandering over skimpy dirt roads and getting lost, Judy had trouble getting into the car to go anywhere unless it was on a macadam road. Informed she might have to spend twenty years at the store before they paved a road out there, she decided to give it a go. We then set out for the main highway that runs between Nairobi and Mombasa.

On our way back to civilization, we saw zebra, gazelles, wildebeests, ostriches, giraffes, and Maasai grazing their cattle. We saw it all from the safety of our car and we enjoyed that fact. One Maasai girl herding cattle let us take her picture and took a pack of cookies for her trouble. We will always have a warm regard for those people. It is said that they have resisted modern ways more than most other Africans. They are a fine, noble people for whatever they believe.

Reaching the Mombasa highway, we stopped for gas and spent some time in a bar. We enjoyed a cold beer and the scene of young people dancing to the soft strains of African popular music. Taking note of us, they played a Western type song they figured we would enjoy. We felt it was very polite of them. They gave us titles of their music found at Kikuyu Records and Disco Music in Nairobi. Sawa Sawa is one title I recall.

We noticed a man sitting at one of the benches, wearing what appeared to be Maasai style clothes draped over his shoulder. He looked Maasai and wore the tire-tread sandals, too. I asked George if he was one of our friends. He didn't know, but we bought him the biggest Tusker beer they had in stock. A glowing smile spread over the man's face as he saluted us in thanks.

We felt good. Those people had a telepathic way of knowing things. Maybe in some way they knew how great our appreciation for a kindness rendered to strangers in need would always be.

Leaving that little wayside bar, we made our way into Nairobi and the Hilton Hotel. We didn't realize how scruffy we were until we looked into the mirrors of our rooms. Luckily, we were able to enter from the garage. The beach towels we washed in the bathtub made the water brown a few times over. How good was it to take a shower? Let me count the ways...

After a day or two in luxury, we caught a flight to Mombasa. From the airplane, we caught wonderful glimpses of Mount Kilimanjaro. I guessed that was as close as we'd ever get. With a touch of sadness at our own misadventures with the Maasai, I wondered: would we trade what we experienced for what we should have seen? I cried real tears six months later when I re-read the story I had sent home to my family. We were exceedingly lucky to have come out of it so well, because we heard of some who were lost in Africa and never seen again.

The Diani Reef hotel sat beside the Indian Ocean in Mombasa. A warm body of water with masses of sea-weed littering the beaches and tangling around the ankles, made the Indian Ocean less than refreshing. When we ventured into the water, it was warm and sort of weedy. However, from the porticos of our rooms it looked wonderful.

Going among the tourists was interesting as well. Many Germans seemed to love it at Mombasa and made their presence felt. You didn't stand in their path unless you liked being bulldozed out of the way.

The sight of the numerous and unusual Boa Bab trees became a great delight for me. I'm sure my companions wondered at my ecstatic rapture over an unusual tree. These trees are massive around the lower trunk but dwindle into a few scraggly branches near the top. Storage rooms, jails, and such are carved out from the insides of these trunks when needed. They seem to grow well in this semi-arid tropical setting, and were scattered about eve-rywhere.

Outside of a great ride on a catamaran, my best memories of Mombasa were those trees, the Germans, and the warm, sea-weedy waters of the Indian Ocean.

Back in Nairobi, I accepted a dinner invitation from an Italian who'd sold a soap factory to the Kenyans. Aldo was a small man and very charming. He ordered a wonderful meal for us, and I will always remember the Italian wine he ordered for dinner. I don't care for wine, but I have to say, it was wonderful. Later on, just as things were getting interesting, I told him, "We have to be at the airport in an hour." With that, I left him saying, "Thanks for a lovely evening, Aldo."

Before we left the airport the Kenyans asked us to cash in all our coins because it is expensive for them to manufacture new coins and they try to hold on to them. Judy and I said goodbye to George as he awaited his flight to England. We flew home to Saudi on a beautiful, clean Saudia plane.

Chapter 12

Caring for Royalty

Why they asked for me I never knew, but a high ranking member of the royal family needed a private nurse for a short time. I should say, a private nurse around the clock was not so much needed, as wanted, expected, and demanded.

A part of caring for this royal patient demanded total security. Thus her care required the use of two wings, one each from two adjoining wards. This formed a large T, with guards placed at all three entrances, and provided the required security.

When royalty or other high officials are admitted to the hospital, the usual amenities afforded those of greater importance when they were admitted were present, spaced conveniently along the halls. They said that a few years earlier, when King Khalid's heart condition demanded it, all patients were removed from coronary care to allow him total privacy. Where those patients on life-sustaining machines were placed they didn't say. Of course, we knew without question, their lives were held in far less importance than that of the king.

Because of his precarious state of health, this king had a 747 fitted out as a hospital ship for his personal use, should he need care while in flight. King Khalid died before we came to Saudi Arabia and Fahd had become the king.

My royal lady patient took possession of a large area that would have held at least twelve or more patients. Each ward is T-shaped. Two legs of the T from each ward had been taken over for this patient. Two rooms were used for dining, one for the royal patient and her personal staff, and one for the myriad of servants in attendance. Her daughter, Soraya, had her own room. The patient herself had her own personal Pakistani nurse and her seamstress, who I took to be a close friend. They all bunched up for the night in that room.

Another room contained a dialysis unit for her personal need. A room was provided for the American doctor and nurse team that administered this care three times weekly to the royal lady.

Her complaint, which was a rather a minor one, being a mild form of eye surgery. Surgical removal of a cataract, and subsequent lens implant, could not be taken care of until an existing problem, a chronic ear infection had been alleviated. Her condition required hospital staff to administer her medications, take vital signs, and chart her progress and condition.

Another duty for me as her nurse appeared to be passing out Tylenol to any and all of her friends and relatives if they requested the medication. Allergies? That never came into question during my time there, but luckily no one had a problem.

Our standard practice on the Saudi wards when any antibiotics, especially of the penicillin strains, were ordered was to give each patient a pre-pen skin test. This test is not known in the US according to doctors I have questioned. But in a population who largely have no knowledge of medicine at all or of allergies, prevention of an allergic reaction is required. When the test reaction proved negative, ie: no redness, swelling or shortness of breath appeared within about twenty minutes, the report went to the pharmacy and the order was filled.

The hallways contained washtubs filled with fresh cut flowers. Amenities carts sat at intervals along the corridors for refreshments such as hot tea, coffee, cider, and flavored drinks. They also contained cookies of many kinds with the Danish buttery ones predominating. Anyone could avail themselves from it any time, day or night.

No doubt a private nurse wasn't necessary, but royalty demanded all the extras. I put in the ear drops and gave

any other meds as ordered. The royal lady had fired one
of her nurses. This ICU nurse's attitude had managed to
relay the feeling that she thought this was nonsense. She
was replaced with an American LPN of lesser training.
That nurse told me, "I put a stethoscope around my neck
and she calls me *doctura.*" Allowed to stay, she did her
shifts without a problem.

My shift, the night shift, usually a quieter time, saw
continued activity since sleep was far from their minds.
The lady had tons of royal visitors. They were dressed to
the nines every night, which in itself, creating a dazzling
array of French haute couture.

The men of the Saudi Royal Family were often very
tall. The lady herself was a very small woman, but her
two sons came in often to see her. They were the epitome
of the handsome Arab prince. Both were well over six
feet four and very handsome. Their wives had an aura of
incredible beauty as well. They wore the finest of Parisi-
an fashions and wore them well. Every night was a veri-
table fashion parade. They were gracious women and
seemed very happy with their lives.

Their husbands allowed them to uncover their faces
during their visits but they all wore the abaya and full facial veiling when entering or leaving the ward. The royal
wives had a way of wearing their scarves that were twisted on the top to form a small sort of tiara which added to
their elegance. I must say I was never bored during that
hitch.

The daughter, a royal princess, who was not as well favored as the royal wives, bore a close family resemblance to her father. All night long, her Filipino maid ran up and down the long halls fetching things for her mistress. The little maid frequently asked me about the United States. She hoped to go there one day and I certainly understood her longing. She was little more than a slave in her present position. The poor girl slept only when her mistress slept and ran her legs off the remainder of the time.

Finally, the doctor decided the royal lady was ready for her eye surgery. She followed her pre-op instructions to the letter, but refused to be taken to the OR via stretcher and insisted upon a wheel chair. I wheeled her to the OR and, as I left her to the care of the OR personnel, I whispered in her ear, "*Fi aman Allah, Madam.*" This is the Saudi version of, "Go with God."

Her surgery went well. I had cautioned her not to bend over in doing her devotions soon after her surgery, as it might increase the intraocular pressure of her eyes and possibly do damage to the surgery. Nevertheless, she was back doing her prayers on the floor by the next day, as all Saudis do who are physically able. I was sure my Arabic was not good enough for proper instructions, but I had brought this problem to the forefront in report. The hospital abounds with Arab speakers who could explain things more clearly than I with my imperfect knowledge of the language.

After her recovery, fat envelopes were passed out to each of us. Within a few days, the lady left via the hospital-equipped, royal 747 to recuperate at Cannes. The royal family has a palace there.

This lady was one of the nicest royals I cared for. She took a personal interest in me to the extent of asking after my family, children, and such things. The experience remains one of the most pleasant I had in the Kingdom.

Chapter 13

My Roommate

Alicia was a beautician before becoming a nurse. As many do who become bored with the everyday routine of nursing, she came to Saudi. She was tiny, very trim, and took exceptional care of her clothing, hair, and looks. At home, she had two teen age children who apparently had a wide variety of mental issues. Why she left them with relatives to embark on an adventure into this strange new world is beyond me—and most anyone who knew her. But there were many others who did the same. Perhaps they had tired of the demanding role of motherhood. Who knows?

Quickly fitting herself into the dating scene, she found it a fertile field for her needs. She always presented a wonderful picture to any interested gentleman, and there were many. She took up scuba diving, rock climbing, and made many acquaintances with people taking part in those adventures. These activities gave me the feeling she wanted to live the dashing life of an international mover and shaker.

At a fancy-dress party, she invariably dressed as a floozy, sporting a tight fitting dress, wearing heavier-than-usual make up, and holding a cigarette in a long lorgnette. Her fluffy red hair completed the picture. Her actions came readily to her in that guise and she had a ball acting the part.

Sometimes at home, she let her guard down, worrying over her children, her inadequacies as a mother, and wondering if she would ever find the right man. Sometimes she had me do a perm for her. We would talk during that time, and I listened, but I really had no good advice for her.

She attracted some very high profile men. One in particular was an Air Force officer. The man, though married, seemed to care greatly for her. But in this case, what could come of their relationship? Eventually, it became one of unhappiness and disappointment. She also found time for a few other relationships on the side. At work she kept the IV fluids running and was good at her job.

Alicia took her vacations alone for the express purpose of meeting men in different countries. In Istanbul, she met a handsome Egyptian and had a torrid relationship for as long as they had the time. Apparently, he invited her to come home with him to Cairo. She followed the man to his home, located outside Cairo on a small farm belonging to his family. There, a huge dose of reality struck her when dirt from the roof overlaid on palm fronds, kept sifting down on them when they were in the home.

I will not soon forget the sight of her sitting neck deep in the bathtub with a dark grayish scum, leaves and sticks, floating around her. She had everything but crawling insects in that water. Her radiant hair, dulled by dirt as well, had to be scrubbed for a long time to get it clean. Generally a fastidious person, she was repulsed by the experience.

I couldn't help wondering how the Egyptian people survived all these centuries living that rustic way. Most of them did, and apparently still do. With the infested Nile river water they drink, the infant death rate must be high.

Later, after she was home for a while, Alicia met the Air Force officer for a date. She slowly returned to her normal state, but not until she discovered she had given the officer a healthy dose of crabs. She had them as well. She sought treatment at our health clinic and I am sure he did the same at his. This did not break them up, however, only his transfer orders did that.

When that day came, they cried together and Alicia certainly cried separately. It was the same old story of dating in Riyadh, meeting someone nice, having an intense relationship, and parting forever when the time came. Judy and I saw it happen over and over. It happened to us.

In time, Alicia found another great guy and went on with her life in Riyadh. She finally found another apartment and moved away. That made room for Judy to move in. We were to become very close friends. We saw Alicia from time to time and talked at work or on the phone, but our lives went different ways.

Chapter 14

On Hash

The Brits have a fancy name for just about everything; its *petrol* for gasoline, *articulated-lorry* for a semi-truck. It's *bloke* for a male friend, or foe, or *on hash* for hiking trips, and so on. For want of something better to do, organized hikes into the desert during the milder months were put together. This sport was new to us, but nothing new to the Brits. They seem to be well organized as a people and hash certainly turned out to be a well thought out event.

With the winter weather so benevolent, we eagerly went on hash many times. Attendees usually numbered into the 50s or 60s at least. Families brought their children and no one went out from the starting point without registering. Conversely, no one ever left the area after the hike without signing back in upon return. Being lost in the Saudi Desert would be a terrifying experience, with its miles upon miles of sand, haze, and nothingness.

Our Arizona desert is filled with many and varied plants, and it is the only desert in the world so favored. The Saudi desert is not a kind place. Descriptions often include: fierce, hostile, bleak, extremely arid, and a very dangerous place in which to be lost. One quickly gains respect for the hardy nomads who have lived here and multiplied for untold centuries.

The colors we are used to seeing in Arizona—pinks, mauves, violets, purples, and all the shades there-of, as well as a clear blue sky—are not seen in the Saudi desert. It has many of the same formations, such as buttes and mountains, but the colors are primarily sandy, dull beige, and chocolates muted together in a never ending scene of desolation.

Most anywhere in nature can be called beautiful if you have enough water and know where you are, but that wild beauty can quickly become a death-trap if you are lost without supplies and transport.

The blue of the Saudi sky is found only in the very highest reaches with shades of sand and beige reaching upward to it. The dunes blow endlessly and shift about, causing some of the finer particles to rise upon the wind.

Our hikes were planned in areas without heavy sand dunes, but out across windswept, rocky ridges and gullies. They say the sand of Saudi Arabia is so rounded that regular sand has to be imported to use in making cement products. Perhaps that is why they can use it so readily for washing themselves. It wouldn't scratch.

The route of one prescribed hike had been planned out in advance and carefully described to the participants. Once on the hike, we easily understood why the precautions for our safe return had been put into place. People took off and spread out, forming more personal groups, according to the people of their acquaintance as well as meeting someone new. Happy voices chatting with their hiking friends as well as juicy snatches of gossip were heard flowing on the warm desert winds.

The rocks and formations were rough and one had to step carefully to avoid an injury. A few leathery-leafed desert trees grew here and there in rock depressions or on the sand. Calling them trees is very generous, considering their torturous and twisted shapes. It would be hard to say if they were ever useful to man. We saw snake holes and tracks of rodents as well. We didn't want to run into any of the snakes for fear they would be deadly.

Frequently, off in the distance, we saw young Saudi men watching the activities of the hikers with their telescopes lens glinting in the sun. For certain, they were hoping to catch a glimpse of unclothed female legs. Sometimes they would be caught sitting around our Olympic sized swimming pool for the same reason. Once discovered, they were asked to leave. The ladies mostly wore shorts on our hikes, so those young boys had some choice viewing if they had spy glasses and, by the metallic glimmering, we knew they did.

Later, as the sun dipped low, we signed back in and waited until everyone had been accounted for. Sometimes there was a worry that someone had been lost out there, but usually it was a forgetful hiker who didn't sign in.

After all were accounted for, they poured green Kool-Aid or whatever it was over some of the people who managed the hash. After that we usually went to someone's villa and had a party and food.

One child stands out in my mind above all others. He was a stocky little British boy with red hair, and he was into everything. He couldn't have been more than four years old, and his mother had her hands full with him. She ran constantly trying to keep him out of trouble.

At these get-to-gathers after the hash, if it got too quiet, someone began throwing people into the pool. We'd move back a ways to be safe, but many didn't want to be safe and ended up screaming in the water. We had wonderful fun until it became time to get home before midnight or be locked out of our compound.

We also had hospital-sponsored outings to the red sands, where we ate and climbed about the red dunes of ancient sand blown into graceful curved forms by the vagaries of the winds.

Buses took us many places, including a trip for desert diamond hunting. We soon became tuned in to finding these soapy glowing stones lying all over this Arabian Nafud desert. These have the same look as real diamonds when you find them and also after they are cut. They look absolutely marvelous, but after having them carefully cut in Bangkok, Thailand, and mounted down in the gold souks by one of the many goldsmiths sitting in a dark corner with his blow torch, you find they soon wear down and become dull and lifeless.

Far better, were the trips to hunt for desert diamonds with our friends. Someone always had a forbidden wonder for everyone to sample or taste depending on the surprise. On one diamond hunting occasion, the big treat one party had brought along and passed all around—was *special meat* and that was pork!

Twenty full grown Westerners standing around munching on a bit of roast pork—this remains in my mind as about the silliest and most fun ever had on an outing. It was all because pork was forbidden in this Muslim country.

Chapter 15

Jilly

Jilly, a nurse from Canada that I knew casually, and I decided on a trip together. We'd attended many of the same parties and got along well enough. Travel in the Middle East is often chancy, and buying tickets from someone called Mr. Swami made it doubly so. Planning an Easter vacation on Cyprus seemed like a great idea. Jilly and I got our leave and with our exit-re-entry visas stamped on our own passports, we happily went to the airport.

All went well until we arrived in Amman, Jordan where we joined a small crowd of anxious passengers clamoring for seats on our flight to Cyprus. After all, we had a condo and a rental car waiting. Shortly, we learned that nineteen of us had bought tickets for seats that did not exist. After an hour of watching a big-nosed ticket agent trying his best to tactfully tell us all to go to hell, I longed for a fluffy haired American girl ticket agent to tick around on her computer and find us seats on that flight or another flight to Cyprus. We found no such luck in the Middle East.

Eventually, a Saudia agent came to our rescue. After endless haggling in Arabic with the Jordanian ticket agent, he said, "I make arrangements for you at hotel for this night. Tomorrow, you must make new arrangements." I thought he said we would be taken to the Holiday Inn. "It has four stars," he assured us.

"Oh well, Holiday Inns are nice and I'm tired," I said, thinking of the nice amenities at a Holiday Inn and trying not to think of the empty rooms awaiting us in Cyprus.

Jilly, fuming, gritted her teeth and her black eyes flashed fire. "That bastard, Swami, knew this all the time!" She droned on, "I wonder how many of these people bought tickets from that slimy S.O.B?"

Crowded onto a small bus, we whirled about the darkened streets of Amman. Arriving at the hotel, we saw it was the Hala Inn, not the Holiday Inn. We voiced our concerns about this.

Our Saudi advocate quickly proclaimed, "Same stars, same stars." We found it barely adequate, but, as the

Saudia man had readily warned us, he really had no obligation to help us at all.

We only had our carry-on bags, so we weren't burdened with luggage. It was on its merry way to Cyprus. Our stuffy rooms contained two beds, each about two feet wide. Jilly had a room just down the hall from me.

Downstairs, in the coffee shop, we were treated to coffee, Arabic bread, and four kinds of falafel by three very cordial Jordanian men. We sat in a booth across from them. They offered to take us to the airport in the morning, but said there would be no more airline tickets available to Cyprus during the Easter Holiday. It seemed everyone knew that but us, and that included Mr. Swami.

Going up to my room, I found myself squeezed into a very small elevator with two Saudi men. A tall, hooded man looked into my eyes with deep, penetrating, and glittering black eyes, and asked, "Are you alone?" His voice, soft, low, and deep, scared me to death. He was hunting for a woman.

I quickly said, "No, I am with my husband." For that reason, I knew I wouldn't spend the night alone in my room with men like that roaming around. I spent the night in Jilly's room for my own peace of mind. Her twin beds were the same restrictive size as the ones in my room.

The next morning, our Jordanian friends took us to the office of the Greek airlines, Olympia Airways. We bought tickets to Athens and our benefactors happily drove us to the airport. They never made a pass at us but only extended their friendship. Those men proved to be helpful Jordanian citizens and certainly a credit to their country. How different from Saudi men. We had no men with us, and the Jordanians offered help without becoming predatory.

Looking back, I believe we were very lucky. Athens at Easter time is a wonderful place. The city bustled with celebratory preparations. We walked through the Plaka. It is a very busy, rather archaic marketplace. Best of all, we looked up and noticed it sat just below the high promontory that holds the greatest ruins in Athens, the Acropolis.

We saw sheep butchered and ready for sale, pig carcasses being carried about on wide shoulders, and people buying clothing and gifts. People were in a joyous mood, rushing about, laughing, and calling out to friends. It created a joyous atmosphere and certainly lightened our mood. We forgot all about Cyprus during our stay in Athens.

Each of the three days leading up to Easter, a somber band marched around a large city square, their instruments blaring sorrowful music. On the last day, six very tall, handsome, Greek men wearing white Grecian outfits, marched at the forefront of the band, as they played triumphant music in celebration of Christ's rising from the dead. At least that was our interpretation of what we saw. Whether I understood it all or not, it remains in my mind as a time of total enchantment.

We had a very reasonable hotel, but no clothes. Shopping in Athens became another Greek experience. I bought shoes—and had my legs felt from the knees down while trying them on. The men were very flirty, but it seemed a fun game to them, and I bought three pairs of shoes. Perhaps it was expected, as part of the sale. I bought a coat, too, but no touchy-feelie for that purchase.

We toured some of the ancient ruins of Greece while we waited for a flight to Cyprus. I took a walk in the Queen's Garden which is huge and beautifully put together with ancient old trees and shady walkways. There were many benches to linger on, and a few overly friendly males trying to get acquainted. They offered their services, but not really threatening in their overtures. I don't remember being afraid like I was of the Saudi man in his woman hunting mode. Apparently, the Greek males don't see women as little better than goats or sheep.

We visited the Acropolis, Syndagma Square and went up the funicular railway to the top of a hill overlooking Athens. We ate there. It is called *Lycobettos* and looks out over Athens where many bits and pieces of ancient ruins dot the landscape. Ancient Greece has been covered with modern Greece. But old ruins, poking up just about everywhere, told of the many civilizations gone before. It gave us the feeling of how life flows on and on, though we, ourselves, do not.

On *Lycobettos* we noticed two British men having the time of their lives. They had no women with them, and possibly never wanted any, but they had a great time seeing Greece. We saw them frequently at other places and the parades as well. They joked with every breath and laughed most of the time. It lifted our spirits watching them. We laughed with each other because of their sense of fun.

Easter Sunday passed, and we easily purchased tickets to Cyprus. There was no problem now and our luggage awaited us there when we arrived. By now we knew we hadn't needed so much anyway. We got the car and Jilly drove us to our flat. They drive the English way and I thought we wouldn't live to get there, driving on the wrong side of the road like that!

The next day, I went to a travel office to book tickets to Alexandria, Egypt on the next cruise ship—big surprise!!

The agent informed me, "There are no cruise ships for another two months, and no flights available now, and for several weeks from now. Your only way off Cyprus is on a Russian Freighter, the S. S. Adjaria. It takes passengers and is currently docked at Larnica. It sails the Mediterranean Sea once each month and stops at Alexandria. It sails tomorrow afternoon. Larnica is across the island and you'll have to find your own ride over."

Frantic at this news, I ran to find Jilly and inform her of this new development.

We quickly bought tickets on the S. S. Adjaria with the home port of Odessa, Russia. Then, driving back to our condo, something went wrong with the car and we gave it back.

The next morning, we found a ride with someone going to Larnica. Before we left, a man proposed marriage to me. I think it was the kohl I had on my eyes. Maybe he thought I was an Egyptian woman. Who knows?

We were packed like sardines in a car whirling wildly over rough roads, but we made it to the seaport. Cypriots drive like the Italians, fast and erratic, and laugh a lot while they do it. On the way, the subject of the partition of Cyprus came up.

The man told us. "The Turkus, dey take it!"

In his voice lay the message that the Cypriots felt they had no chance of ever regaining the other half of their island from the Turks. They felt the island nation of Cyprus would be divided with a high fence for many years to come. Not only that, it sounded like it could be very dangerous to cross over to that side as well.

We came to the waterfront in Larnica and saw our ship sitting dockside boasting the hammer and sickle on their red flag, a daunting sight for us.

Before we boarded, I changed my Cyprus money for U.S. money from a passerby. It wasn't much, only five dollars, but it came in handy on our voyage. We toted our own luggage and set it on the deck which looked splintery and sun-bleached white. Immediately, a pert little Russian woman stepped up and asked for our passports and we had no choice but to surrender them—once again!

Our cabin, in the hold about three levels down, made us realize we had neglected to purchase first class accommodations. We couldn't begin to imagine what class these were. The bunks were narrow, the toilet and bathroom were communal and down a long, narrow hall.

When the ship moved out of port, we stood on deck watching the red hammer and sickle flag wave over the end of the ship, an experience I never imagined I'd ever have. Had I not already been in the Middle East for over two years, I think I would have been out of my mind with fear, finding myself in a situation like this.

The Arab was correct when he said, "Americans are not thinking bad." We do not suspect the worst of anyone in general and these were just people, too. We never really worried at all.

Soon, a sailor began haranguing us in Russian about our luggage. No one offered us a hand, and we hauled it down to our room. Later, when they washed the deck with sea water, we realized the sailor had tried to be helpful, but without helping, of course.

In the dining room, we were told where to sit, and you'd better not try to change places as this area had a little female commissar ruling over it. Any infraction was met with narrowed eyebrows, a stern face, and pointing finger. A Syrian man tried to change places to sit near Jilly. He never made it, as she pointed to his seat saying, "You sit there!" He didn't quibble with her and, chagrinned, the amorous gent slunk back to his assigned seat.

Not being a good sailor, my stomach was not up to eating, though I tried. Russian fare on this cruise left much to be desired. Everything looked to have been boiled or washed clean of any sort of taste. The drink, an orange-smoky looking concoction, had little or no taste and was not drinkable either. They served our food in courses. First, a tiny bit of fish on a limp green leaf, then noodles with boiled meat, bread, potatoes, and last, a paste-like dessert. I noticed Jilly ate well enough, but I scarcely managed a hundred tasteless calories.

After dinner, we relaxed to the evening's entertainment. Many passengers sat around in a large salon. The only ones who looked like they might speak English were Germans, and they didn't. As we sat together, we noticed we tended to drift toward those who looked more like us. We sat with the Russian sailors and the Germans. The more Middle-Eastern looking passengers sat on the other side.

The entertainment consisted of American commercials, or at least English language ones. Everyone enjoyed them to no end. Some Middle Eastern girls got up and did a dance, see-sawing back and forth. It looked very graceful, but one I had never seen before or since. They did a nice job of it. For sure, they weren't Saudi girls.

I pocketed my dessert at one meal, being too sick to eat it. In the middle of the night, they stopped at Latakia, Syria. The ceasing of motion brought on an unbelievably raging hunger, and I enjoyed the Russian version of a lady finger. It was four inches wide, six inches long, and about an inch thick. It wasn't very sweet, but oh, how good it was! I got slimmer every day on that voyage.

The ship stopped at Arab ports and took on additional passengers. On deck, after that, we were besieged with Arab women trying to bum stuff from us. They got my orange and some of Jilly's cigarettes. It was all we had to give. Below decks, they yelled and chattered in Arabic but we were used to it and paid no heed.

Remember those aluminum curlers with the rubber roller on the ends? While Jilly entertained the Syrian gentleman she'd met on board down in our room, I had my hair done, all by sign language. My Russian lady hairdresser used those same rollers from my childhood.

The beautician, an older woman with a pleasant smile, had parakeets in a cage. She sprayed my hair to a standstill, and it only cost five bucks. I had the chance to enjoy a real one on one experience with a very pleasant Russian lady.

Later, Jilly glowingly related to me how well-endowed the Syrian man had been. She never missed a chance to down grade Americans, but my own opinion of her wasn't so great, either. Though she was a Canadian, she tried to feign the British-type superiority over everyone, but it fell flat with me. If she saw someone with wrinkles, or a few bits of lint on their jacket, she would sniff, "Humph, look at that—must be an American. They absolutely don't know how to dress."

Coming to the port of Alexandria, the prim little purser came up with our passports. We had forgotten all about them. We couldn't enter Egypt without them. Was this another incident of Americans 'not thinking bad'?

We were interviewed by the harbor master, a little Egyptian man exuding importance. He made out endless papers before the ship could dock and the disembarking could begin.

Bringing our luggage up from three decks below took a considerable amount of effort, but no man stepped up to assist us. Instead, they all enjoyed themselves standing about watching the *Ameriakias* struggling as we tugged the stuff up on deck. In that instance, it was good they didn't understand English because Jilly's black eyes snapped and her tongue let loose. Actually, she held the worst of the invectives in. At least for her.

Later, at the hotel, they took our passports again. It had become routine. We wondered about their curiosity of females traveling alone. We weren't sure, and they didn't say.

Alexandria should have been a lovely seaside city. But with the streets full of sand and litter, and clothing hanging out to dry from apartment windows, some of the luster went missing. I'll never forget the sight of a beautiful, but emaciated, Arabian horse. It struggled along, pulling a heavy load for his master. His fine lines and bone structure apparently went unseen by his master who only saw him as a beast of burden. The people were poor in this country and seeing the finer side of life likely escapes them in their daily struggle for existence.

Alexandria, Egypt, was very old, and we found a guide who took us to see many old places. There were untold tales of previous civilizations, carvings, and pits half filled with water. Many treasures lay beneath if only the water could be removed. We visited ancient mosques which we were allowed to enter. We saw charming palaces for the wealthier Egyptians. All the historical monuments we saw made us realize how ancient the city of Alexandria was.

We saw many fine sights before we took the train to Cairo. That train, well and frequently used, had to be the dirtiest conveyance in existence. The only sight of the original carpet color was around the legs of the seats where it hadn't been worn or soiled. The toilet was a hole over the tracks and one would never consider sitting down on that thing, no way!

Looking out the dirty, fly-specked, windows, we saw men driving oxen or donkeys around in circles pumping water, or threshing grain. Their mud houses had thatched roofs. No air conditioning there. Occasionally, a camel carried materials or grain stacked high, but mostly donkeys and cattle did the work.

On some of the houses along the way, we saw how they had attended the Hajj, or pilgrimage. Moslems are importuned to make this trip to Mecca at least once in their lives. If they do make the pilgrimage, in some countries, the journey is remembered by painting the modes of travel used to get there on their homes. Egypt was one of those countries where the trip was proudly displayed in pictures painted on the sides of their home.

In Cairo, we found a teeming city with streets clogged with cars, horses, carts, and casually tossed refuse. Our room at the Ramses Hilton, on the 10th floor, did not prevent the odors of the city from wafting up to us on the dry desert air.

From there, we found our way to the National Museum where King Tut's sarcophagus is located, just behind the Nile Hilton, about a hazardous, auto-clogged, city block away. The place held hundreds of sarcophagi that had been salvaged from the multitude of burial sites. It seemed haphazard to us, but they exuded obvious pride in that part of their history, as well they might.

After dinner, the evening's entertainment held our fascination as well. A Yemini man was selected by a female entertainer and was subsequently humiliated by her act. He was mortified. He didn't understand that it was just a show.

We talked to him the next morning, trying to make him understand the situation and help him feel better. We soon realized he thought we wanted his personal attention, and we quickly drifted away.

We did notice that anytime a man in Saudi national dress came on the scene, he received royal treatment.

That white thobe and red patterned gutra head dress, or a white one, worked wonders everywhere in Egypt.

We wanted to tour the pyramids. Everyone always knows someone who will be a wonderful guide. After bargaining for the price, we set out. Jilly rode the camel and I rode a very thin Arabian horse. Our guide referred to the Sphinx, as 'the spinkus.' He obviously took no real pride in his national treasures, but he did know how to work us for extra money.

Later, we changed mounts and were separated on the way back. The kid who led my camel put the bite on me for extra *baksheesh*, or he wouldn't take me back. Angered, I said, *"La—anna imshee"* or, "No—I will walk," and started to slide off. He quickly recanted and led the camel back, which was a good thing as that camel was very high.

I complained about it when we returned. The man walked up to the boy and slapped him hard across the face. His action shocked us, though we realized the boy had been caught at an extra shake-down.

Then, as an act of contrition, the man set us up to buy a cartouche in eighteen karat gold, at a reduced price, with our names on them in ancient Egyptian hieroglyphics. We bought them. Later, comparing notes, we found that Jilly had paid the man for our tour around the pyramids and the 'spinkus' and so had I. Lessons learned too late! We had a good laugh over it.

We flew up the Nile to the Valley of Kings in an air-bus containing mostly Germans. They must travel a lot. We tried our best to be careful of what we ate, but on a tour to see the unfinished obelisk, Jilly collapsed on a rock and could not get up. A kind of stomach flu had hit her that fast and that hard. The Nubian guide and I poured her into the car, and I took a few quick pictures of the huge obelisk. It lay on its side where it had cracked before they finished it, and it was left in situ.

At the hotel, I despaired for Jillly's life for a while. But sick or not, we had to take a train for Cairo at midnight. With help, we got her on board and during the trip we received many offers of medical help. By morning, as we hit the train station, Jilly was well enough to get off the train and carry her luggage up to the station. They made us get off so far away she had to walk a long distance over railroad tracks and gravel sidings. She pulled her own luggage, and the poor, sick woman had a struggle making it.

We took a cab and asked the driver for a pharmacia. After explaining Jilly's condition to him, the pharmacist gave me Belladonna and an antibiotic for her, and we went on to the airport.

At the Cairo airport I watched cats cavorting around on people's luggage while Jilly laid down on a handy bench. We found out our flight on Egypt Air took us to Dhahran before going to Riyadh. Worse yet, we had hours yet to wait. I found a Saudia man, explained the situation to him, and he said, "Come, bring your friend and your luggage."

I dragged Jilly over to him along with our luggage. He put us on one of their clean, cool planes and we were on our way to home to Riyadh within an hour. Later, I discovered that the Egyptian revenge had affected me, too, but not as bad as Jilly.

Chapter 16

At Work

Gossip made the rounds on nursing wards in The States, but in Saudi, it was the life's blood of social and useful news. We learn of parties, happenings on other wards, and sometimes dire facts of importance. Information on the television was glossed over and prettied to make all things seem wonderful.

Judy came onto this shocker by way of good old gossip.

It came to Jude's ears that Idi Amin, a patient at King Faisal, had taken quite a fancy to a beautiful, blonde, American, ICU nurse. He must have verbalized his desire for her, and someone overheard him. How much danger she was in, we had no way of knowing, but it had to have been substantial. Her rescue was as dramatic as any heard of in the Kingdom. What he indicated toward her regarding his intentions was not revealed, and those things will never be known but to the lady and those involved in her rescue.

Imagine being sought for sexual pleasure by one of the world's most despotic, evil men. A paunchy man, dissolute in habit and responsible for the torturous deaths of about 500,000 thousand of his countrymen. As president of Uganda from 1971-1979, his brutal disregard for human rights caused mass executions, chaos, and deepest poverty within Uganda until he was deposed. He became a Muslim after he fled to Libya. Tossed out of there, he fled to Saudi Arabia in 1979. He robbed and dehumanized his people while living in high style, denying himself nothing. Exiled in Saudi Arabia, he resided in a lovely white palace on the outskirts of Jeddah during the time we lived and worked in the Kingdom.

The story of the nurse's escape is that she walked out of the hospital into a U. S. Air Force auto and was whisked away to the airbase. From there she was flown home to The States. Her belongings were packed up and sent home after that. He must have planned her kidnapping and delivery to his white palace outside of Jeddah. From there she would never have escaped. For an American woman or any other woman, her life with that ugly monster would have been one of the deepest despotic hell. A sympathetic Muslim kingdom would have found it difficult to rescue her or prosecute him. That would be if they even knew about her situation.

If she had mysteriously disappeared, would the police have looked for her? Our Embassy—who knows? We were always warned to be careful when we went anywhere.

Work, always interesting in a strange country, was frequently shocking as well. This Middle Eastern culture was thousands of years old, and we continually tried to remember that, but some things would never seem right to Westerners.

Their idea of marriage comes to mind. A patient, Abdullah, a man in his fifties, severely injured in an automobile accident, had lost his wife, or one of his wives in that accident. When asked if he would marry again. He replied, "Oh yes, I have already bought my wife, but I must wait. She is only nine." We tried to hide our shock at this sort of news, knowing that female children are raised to believe this is right, but we felt sick for days afterward just thinking about the fate of that little girl.

Female children at an early age are taught by their female relatives many ways to entice their husbands. I have seen little girls swaying in an overtly sexual manner, giving come hither looks with sultry eyes, and sexily undulating little hips as they hum and sing love songs. They swing their long black hair while they move about as well.

When that little child has her first menses, the man can exercise his rights as a husband and according to an Iraqi psychiatrist we knew, some of these children end up in the mental asylum from the trauma of the marital bed.

Rarely do these Bedouin children attend school or know any other way of life. Raised to be wives and mothers and, with no other option, their up-bringing prepares them for this life. I hoped rather than believed this to be true.

One child of ten comes to mind. Sheika, who had received a kidney from her father, used to dance for us, showing the suggestive moves she knew. Her body, chubby and bloated from the steroids required to prevent rejection of the donor organ, wiggled and swayed along with come hither glances.

She hated her bloated appearance and the stringent diet she was required to follow. Those things had developed a raging hunger within her and she told us she would eat herself to death when she got home.

We experienced other strange occurrences. Saleh, a desert man, and his *mirafic,* or sitter, did not understand water displacement. The *mirafic* drew Saleh a bath. The water level being two inches from the top of the tub meant to me that it was too full and would overflow if he put the patient in there. Before going to lunch, I warned him. Pointing to the floor, I said with my firmest voice, "*Mafi moya hina.*" This meant no water on the floor. I left for lunch.

Upon my return, I found the huge pile of wet towels he had used to mop up what he had spilled. Unable to censor any of them, we got a laundry hamper for the wet towels. I wondered if he would do that particular thing again. Had he learned about water displacement?

Sometimes a father or friend, as the *mirafic,* would bathe the patient. They merely set the patient on the toilet and poured many pans of water over them. This happened in a carpeted bathroom with a walk-in shower right handy. The water drained out onto the carpet or tiled floor, depending on how it was finished. With no bathrooms or running water in the desert, they hadn't learned to deal with running water, plumbing, bathroom fixtures, or bidets either.

They washed with sand more often than not. We learned that from a Filipino nurse who worked at teaching personal care to Bedouin women in the Eastern Sector of Saudi Arabia. She said they laughed at her and told her she was crazy for using water to wash the private parts. Water is too precious to waste in that manner. Sand is used for cleaning.

Sand is also used in their cleansing ritual in preparation for *salat*, or prayer time. Many a patient kept a small box of desert soil or sand at the bedside to use for this. City dwellers use the long washing troughs, placed handy to mosques, for their pre-prayer ablutions. We saw that at every *salat* if we were nearby.

Women were very friendly and allowed photos to be taken, but their overall concern was that, "No man see." We carefully promised this and I have always obeyed that tenant. We would betray them if we allowed a man to gaze upon their features even though it be another country and a later time.

One such woman had survived an auto accident which killed her husband. She had no permanent injuries herself, but her little son did. She remained with us because her four year old son, Abdulraman, had a tracheostomy performed after the accident and it could never be closed because a poorly trained doctor had shoved an emergency endotracheal tube into and through his voice box causing permanent damage. Thus this small child had to have this foreign object tied to his neck at all times and did not understand the need for it.

Nasser was another of our patients having a permanent lifetime tracheostomy due to poor emergency medical treatment as well. Nasser, six years old and a burn victim, spent much time playing with Abdulraman.

More than once Abdulraman pulled out his trach tube. We scrambled frantically to find it and replace it before the opening closed. They tend to close very rapidly so time is of the essence, aside from the fact that he was unable to breathe without this device. Each time this occurred he lost a bit more brain function. We knew his life would be shorter because of it.

The last time this happened, we couldn't find his trach tube. We ran frantically to Nasser's room for his extra sterile one. After restoring Abdulraman's respirations we found he had thrown his trach tube in the garbage. We hadn't thought to look there and it would not have been sterile in any case.

We played with these children as much as possible and soon realized that playing was something new for them. At least having Westerners play with them certainly was. I used to take Nasser in my arms and hold him tight, then spin around with him in one of our office chairs to make him try to squeal with delight, (he was voiceless). He had terrible burn scars, and with a permanent trach, what lay ahead for him?

A woman, Amara, who enjoyed the status of being the only wife of her husband, had extensive female surgery. The doctor carefully explained to the husband that she could not have sexual intercourse for several weeks. He immediately went out and bought another wife.

Learning this, Amara, in her abject misery, wanted to kill herself. She cried for days. We could not help her. She had to accept this new woman in her husband's life, but the glow of pride at being the only wife had left her gentle face.

ოოო

When the Saudis bought goods, they often got a raw deal in their purchases. About the worst, but not a big thing, were the wonderful IV poles sold to them by the Italians. The bases were so small, no bigger than twelve inches in diameter, that if you hung a 1000 cc bag of fluid from the top, the thing would topple over. These unusable poles soon disappeared. Maybe they went with that watered down lotion they got from the United States.

Nagi, a Yemini man, had gotten cancer from chewing *Gat*, the narcotic weed so often used among the poor to allay hunger pangs. The cancer affected his tongue most of all, but also many of the connective tissues in that area. He received Morphine for his pain and his thought processes were frequently off track.

He likely despaired of ever leaving the hospital, since he slowly grew worse, and may not have fully understood how sick he was. His *mirafic* likely didn't either, though they must have seen the results of chewing *Gat* more than once.

The Saudis' hate and disdain over the use of drugs usually meant trouble if caught. But when Nagi got out of the hospital, and into someone's car and drove it into another vehicle, they were very gentle with him. They evidenced a great deal of sympathy for him when they brought him back to us.

Nagi continued to eat as best he could until one evening his tongue fell off into his soup. He became hysterical and had to be put on Valium thereafter. It wasn't much longer after that before we turned his face toward Mecca.

We also received a little high born child—maybe a lesser prince—about the age of four years old. This boy had wandered into the swimming pool and nearly drowned. He'd been resuscitated enough to have decent vital signs, but had not awakened. Thus the prognosis for his recovery was extremely poor. The swimming pool had been neglected and had foul greenish water in it which further afflicted the child's breathing capacity since his lungs were befouled as well.

He came to us at MCF basically for long term care. On his chart, we saw a notation that should he die, the police were to be notified. We knew this meant that the person charged with his care during his childhood would be held responsible for his death. We dreaded to think what this poor soul's fate might be.

The family brought in an older man who held the position of a healer of sorts. He shook an object over the child and spit repeatedly over him from top to bottom. He invoked softly chanted prayers as he worked over the boy. The family stood back, hoping he might be successful. No real spittle touched the child that we could see, and if it had, we would never have interfered. Native medicine has been shown to have power to those who use it and believe in it. It had no effect on this child that we could see.

Later on, they brought in a specialist. A doctor of Indian decent, who carefully examined the child, read his charts, records, and examinations. He then pronounced his findings, "This child has cerebral anoxia."

This means lack of oxygen to the brain. His proud pronouncement may have warranted the price he charged the parents. But this was no news to us, since that had been his admitting diagnosis. The doctor strutted off the floor, and we never saw him again. Generally, a case of severe loss of brain function stays this way until death occurs.

We saw great concern by families for their family members. One example was the case of Saleh. He was a nineteen-year-old boy with a star-shaped tumor on his left knee. His diagnosis was astrocytoma. If an amputation was done very quickly, the chance for survival was improved. This had not been done in Saleh's case since he came from an outside hospital. They didn't practice the level of medicine found at King Faisal.

His mother came to see him after he had spent several weeks with us. When she saw how very ill he was, she never left his side until he died. Her meals were served to her, complements of the hospital. His leg had swollen to a massive size and his pain was monumental. The father came in and out of the room and remonstrated with her trying to make her leave.

She never left the room. She stayed at her son's bedside until we turned his face toward Mecca. She mourned the loss of her son quietly and her pain nearly broke our hearts.

Another case involved a female child with brain cancer, a glioblastoma, the worst possible type. The little girl, about six years old, had lost her hair due to radiation. Her most-beautifully shaped head resembled the head of Nefertiti—tear-drop shaped, and exotically beautiful. The old man who sat with her day and night was her father, though at first I referred to him as her grandfather.

They quickly set me straight about that and I carefully called him *Baba,* which any Arab male may be called. Surprisingly, even a young boy may be called *baba.* It means father. Each time we attended the girl, bathing, turning, or medicating, he would thank us in a voice filled with sorrow and deep meaning. "*Shukran, Sister, shukran.*"

Sadly, the day came when the child had to be transferred to the hospital called Shemaze. By now we knew it was a poor place for a child in her condition. As far as we knew, hands on care was not likely to be given.

How did we know? Because Raymond, a male English nurse we worked with, followed a male patient we had sent there. He went to see the man. He found him still wearing the same gown he'd worn when he'd been transferred to Shemaze two weeks before. Raymond bathed the man, changed his clothes and his bed linens. That was all he could do for him. He was sickened by the care the spotlessly dressed Korean Nurses had provided the poor soul.

We frequently saw these nurses when they brought a patient to King Faisal for specialized treatment. They looked wonderfully professional, but they certainly could not have been up to American or British standards of care.

The Egyptian nurses told us that any personal care given to their patients in Egypt was done by the patient's family. Now we knew why all but a few of the nurses we received from Egypt, were utilized as Nurse II's or nurse's aids on the floors of Faisal. An Egyptian nurse's aide, Fatima, very incensed by her position at Faisal, proudly claimed, "At home I am ICU nurse."

It all depended which school they attended. If they had graduated from the school in Cairo staffed by American and British instructors, they were hired as nurse I's. Otherwise, if taught by Egyptian instructors, they were nurse IIs or aides.

I believed the hospital was right in this. We were told that in the early days of oil exploration, Egyptian doctors ran a clinic for the oil workers. It sounded like something out of a horror movie. We were told they used surgical tools and hung them on the walls after use—without benefit of washing or sterilization.

Injured or ill American and British workers were flown to England, a six hour flight to modern medicine. That sort of medieval clinic no longer existed in Saudi, but stories like that still did and were not flattering to the old Middle Eastern style of medicine.

Sadly, sometimes the care the Saudis sought, and paid highly for, did not meet their expectations or our standards either. An American doctor who had invented a defective heart valve came to Saudi for a hitch. At that time the only country that used his type heart valve happened to be Pakistan. No other country that we knew of allowed the use of it. They were outlawed because of post-operative problems of clot formation. This was always a consideration, but apparently it was much more severe with this valve. This doctor had invented it and was exceedingly proud of it.

Why the man used them in Saudi came as a great surprise to us. We decide it was to further build his ego since the device bore his name. That he stayed a month or two longer than the other doctors only added to the heartache. He unfailingly used this defective valve in every patient he operated on. Later on, we were to see the final result of this sort of treatment.

The operating nurses told us that during one valve replacement surgery he boldly verbalized his expertise on a young Saudi man during his operation to receive a new aortic valve. Explaining the different tissues of the heart as he prepared this man's heart to receive the new valve, he scooped out tissue to be excised. Only it happened to be the tissue needed to sew the new valve in place. This patient died on the operating table. When the doctor left the operating theater, he refused to speak to the patient's family. They had waited patiently outside for their loved one to come out and for the doctor to tell them everything went well.

They said he stormed out saying, "What more do they want from me?"

We listened to this in shock and shame for our country. This doctor stayed a few extra weeks and no telling what else happened under his surgical knife.

A year later we saw the result of this sort of valve. We never knew if this woman had that particular valve or not, but her problems of clotting were very severe. Multitudes of tiny clots flowed through her bloodstream. She was medicated with anticlotting medication.

She was scheduled for another valve replacement, but they had to wait because she had infected teeth. Infections of this sort will also infect a new heart valve. They took her off the anti-clotting medication to fix her teeth. She threw massive clots to the brain before she had the valve replacement.

We received her in MCF for long term care. She was a beautiful young mother of two daughters. Her hair, long, black, and wavy got us into a bit of trouble. We used to sit her in her chair with her freshly washed hair hanging over the back to dry. Unfortunately, too many Saudi men enjoyed the sight as much as we did and we had to cover her face and her hair. We were wrong. We had forgotten ourselves for the moment. Our lady only lived a short time with us before she threw more massive clots and died. This sad incident stayed with us for years.

So many of our patients were unforgettable and their families as well. How often did we receive the invitation to sit on the floor with them and partake of sweet tea and dates? Our patients unfailingly expressed their gratitude for the care they received.

Their attitudes regarding death were varied as well. Amer, one of our aides, became terrified when one of our older patients died. He took one look, walked down the hall, and out the door. His face as white as a tan face can get.

A Saudi man, whose wife Mohamadiah died, merely wrapped her in a clean sheet. He picked her up in his arms and carried her out to the car, put her in the back seat, and drove off.

We knew he had to have her body completely washed by Muslim body washers to remove the taint of us, who are infidels, off her body. She would then be wrapped in a new sheet and buried, all within a one day period. It is said that at least twenty grave sites are kept open in the City of Riyadh at all times for just this purpose since Muslims are to be buried within twenty four hours.

In so many ways, all this made sense to us. How nice not to deal with funeral directors at a time of grief. To have the closeness of familiar local people who care for the dead seems much more comforting somehow.

The royals, at least their kings, are not buried thus. They are carried all about the city on a wooden affair that looks very much like a wooden ladder for all to see the deceased monarch. Then after this ceremonial parading of the body in public, it is then taken far into the desert to be buried in an unmarked grave.

They do not make a practice of embalming the dead, but only wash the remains clean of all taint before burial. We were told the Saudis do not make a practice of visiting their grave sites after burial.

Another thing that crept into my feelings puzzled me. The young children's eyes sparkled and they were quick to learn anything put to them. But we noticed the eyes of the elders had a dead look. I never understood it until I spoke to a woman from Sri Lanka who taught female medical students. We were waiting for the flight to Kuwait. I would be attending the wedding of a friend to an Iraqi man. Where the instructor was headed, I didn't know. But she told me about her work.

"By the time I get these students," she said, "their minds are closed to independent thought by the teachers they've had before me." With a pained expression, she continued, shaking her head. "It is difficult to teach them the freedom of critical thought and ability necessary to deduce solutions to problems."

For a long time I puzzled over her words, but when we received an Arab patient from the Persian Gulf Region who worked for ARAMCO, his eyes were alive and bright, his speech as well. What made that difference, some interaction with the outside world perhaps? I still puzzle over this.

The Saudis claimed to hate the Jews, but Jewish medical people worked in Saudi. One Jewish nurse, from Phoenix, was given charge of our recovery room before her first month was out.

Another incident surprised me one evening. The phone rang and I answered, "MCF, third floor."

"Hello, this is Dr. Horowitz."

"Dr. Horowitz?" I said.

The surprise in my voice was evident.

"Yes—Dr. Horowitz," he replied, understanding my question for what it was.

"Okay doctor, what are your orders?" I asked.

I realized the Saudis didn't know a Jewish name as we might, but recognized only the stamp of Israel on a passport or a shekel or two in your purse. All new maps in the Kingdom had Israel carefully blacked out, no doubt by a member of the religious police. I have one with me at home.

Chapter 17

An Oasis

Judy, two male friends, and I set out to visit a small town about sixty kilometers—or clicks as the guys like to say—out of Riyadh. The road was nicely paved as usual and the scenery was one of near desolation. Along the way, we saw a Foremost Dairy shop that sold ice cream. Nothing else stood around it and we wondered who ever patronized the place.

When we entered the dusty desert town of Al Kharj, we drove around taking a look. We visited a large open air vegetable market. There were great quantities of produce available and we bought fresh fruit and a few vegetables. Sorry, old vehicles lined the main street, well used trucks, and dusty cars. "What a poor little place," I commented.

Near the edge of the town, we saw the huge old ruins of a mud palace. Wandering around the crumbling outer façade, we wondered what things had happened in this old ruin where ancient rulers had held their *majilis* over the years. It's easy to let the imagination run rampant in a place like that.

A *majilis* is the meeting of the rulers with their people. In Saudi Arabia, a man can come before his king and seek justice for his wrongs, real or imagined. It is a good system in that a man can go before his ruler personally to seek recompense with no intermediary or lawyer to muddy up the proceedings. This is one reason the Saudis feel close ties to their monarchy. He is approachable to his people.

In Al Kharj, we discovered the secret of how the Arab had survived over so many eons. This was an oasis—not as in the movies, a waterhole surrounded by sand dunes and a few date palms. This oasis was comprised of hundreds of acres of date palms, fields of grain and vegetables. Livestock grazed in green pastures, and people tended them.

We learned there were several areas in this barren Nafud desert where the underground water flowed near to the surface, creating large fertile areas where food could be grown and sold or traded to passing tribes for useful products they needed. The sight of a real, amply watered, teeming oasis consisting of hundreds of arable acres, answered many questions I had formed in my mind.

Now we knew why this place had once been a great center of activity, warranting the huge mud palace we had seen. There exists a large system of water courses beneath the sands of this country. Oil was valuable, but more than water?

We all bought a *shawarma* from a local vendor, before setting out for Riyadh. This consisted of spicy meat, beef, chicken or lamb roasted on a round moving spit encircled by red hot wires. The cooked meat was sliced off, laced with hot sauce and yoghurt, and placed in a long bun, a generous meal for the price of a couple of Saudi Riyals. This Saudi style fast food was nearly the same as the Greek Gyro sandwich, and the Greeks through the centuries might have learned it from the Arabs. Or vice versa—who knows?

That they bore similar features, I learned from my friend, the Arab. He told me when he was in Greece, he asked an old man, "Why you don't speak Arabic with me?" With puzzled expression, my friend told me, "He look same like me, Arab man, but he speak only Greek."

On our way home, we stopped at the Foremost Ice cream store.

Chapter 18

The C Party

After a year or more, Tessa moved to a newer apartment. This new one used 220 watts electricity, and she needed converters for everything. Since Judy and I had become good friends, I asked her to move into our house. She had been subjected to a series of unpleasant roommates and accepted readily. From then on we attended more parties together.

When the C-party came along, deciding what to wear was the smaller part of preparing for this occasion we were to attend. Having a male escort was, as always, very illegal and the bigger part of any outing. Judy mentioned her date was going as a clock and she, having a flair for the exotic, decided to be Cleopatra. After all, a toga thing would be easy enough. No sewing involved, just a few gold tinted chains and lots of blue eye shadow might just make a very striking costume.

Judy's date had the appearance of a distinguished Englishman. Reginald, as rumor had it, was very much enamored of another. So it would require a bit more inducement on Judy's part to bring him in tow.

After a long day on A 1, I dropped into a chair, and sighed. "What a hell of a day we had. It was either Marama's son sitting in the hall staring at us, or Ablehadi hanging over the desk in his stained thobe. His lower lip is always drooping as he asks for *bunni* (brown or chocolate) ice cream!"

Laughing at my own complaints, I turned my attention to Judy's query about my costume for the C Party. "Because of the leopard print shorts I had bought in Nairobi, my date and I could go as cats if I wear a black top, and make us some ears, and a tail. What do you think?"

"How many days are left to get this done? Yours sounds great, but you know I can't sew a stitch to work on mine."

"How could you possibly have raised six kids, and never learn to sew? I don't believe it."

"I can't sew a button on a shirt—how about that?" Judy laughed and draped several yards of white filmy cloth about her figure. "What about this? If I wear a gold tiara, and lots of gold bracelets, and go heavy on blue eye shadow, I don't need to sew it, just belt it."

Indeed, it did fit her well, and she was about to give Liz Taylor a run for her money in that get-up. Judy, a look-a-like for Crystal Carrington of the TV series Dynasty, managed to belie in every way, her age, or child-bearing history.

I have said so many times that Saudi Arabia proved to be the older woman's dating paradise, and for so many of us that was true. We had dates, all-be-it maybe not with the men of our dreams, but great guys all the same. If you wanted to date, you could. At least there were no bums or losers around. You could not go to Saudi Arabia without a good job, usually a professional position, manager of some sort, technical guy, or at the very least, an engineer.

Our dates worked at a compound which shall remain nameless, but was the most American in amenities and furnishings. They had a big swimming pool, huge dining facilities, and the most American kitchen. It was said an American housewife had decided on the layout and appliances.

Once the night of the party arrived, my date, Larry, came to pick us up in his worn-but-serviceable car. Whenever we arrived at their compound, we always looked across the street to where there was an insane asylum built for Saudi females. It was a large, deep, tan-colored place with strange figures decorating the outer walls at intervals around the sides. I sometimes wondered if the inmates had designed some of those ornate and un-usual designs.

We wondered what might cause them to become af-flicted this way. We had at least one answer from an Iraqi psychiatrist who had treated several cases of young wom-en sold into marriage at an age so young they had not be-gun their menstrual cycles.

When that event occurred, the marriage would be consummated whether the bride was willing or not. In one case he told us, the mother held her daughter down while the husband completed the act. The child was judged deranged from the trauma and placed in the men-tal facility. Considering the tender, young age when men-arche (the first menstrual cycle) usually begins in warmer climates, it boggles the mind to imagine the fear and pain the poor young girl suffered. Of course, the young bride belonged to him in every way. We wondered if he saw her as a life mate, or just wanted the pleasure of a very young female. Certainly, he would expect children as well.

Shivering at the barbarity of what would be to us, child molestation, we tried to see it in the light of customs held by an ancient people. This was a difficult task at best. We turned away from that building across the street and went inside with our friends to relax, eat dinner, and have a sip of whatever brew these guys had concocted.

Living areas provided by the Saudi's are referred to as compounds. They usually were surrounded with high fences as well. These were, almost without exception, busy places in the making of alcoholic products and it went on continually. Occasionally, a warning would go out via the grapevine that there was to be an inspection by the government for illegal substances. At such times it would have been unwise to strike a match near a toilet for fear of an explosion. Everything went down the drain. When the danger died down, the brewing began all over again, and a party was held when there was enough exotic substance to go around.

Larry and I were ready to go as jungle cats, with whiskers, tail, claws, and leopard print shorts. Judy and Reginald were set as well. He sported a white T-shirt with clock numerals and big and little hands and a pendulum. He made very certain that the long hanging pendulum hung and swung down in the most important place, adding a little risqué flip to the hilarity of the evening. His lady, all decked out in her finery, looked so much like Liz Taylor in the movie Cleopatra, that she was an instant and busy success. Were her feet worn out by night's end? They were.

At the party we met people we knew and many we didn't. We were told after the party that there was a Saudi present. If he was, he didn't stand out as one. I wondered how he felt about the curriculum presented by the cheer leaders, Fritzie, an American, and Martin, a free-wheeling Englishman. At times during the evening they would do a few cheers and hand out their college course availabilities.

Mentioned among them were: 101 ways to Flip your *Gutra.* Another course was called, Decapitation, or How to Lose 12 Ugly Pounds Instantly. It also mentioned day-glow clothing, or see through *thobes*, and many, many others. Few of these were complementary to the Saudis. We wondered if the Saudi guy would turn us in and we'd all be kicked out of the Kingdom.

Fritzie and Martin had a long and very intense relationship during their years over there. They had their favorite musical group, their records, and always danced well together. I believe they liked the "Platters" the most. They often held small intimate dinners and were wonderful hosts. Martin, was married, but like so many others over there, he sought feminine companionship.

One tall man had dyed a thobe red and came as a Cardinal of the Catholic Church. Another pinned ladies' under-panties to his chest and came as a chest of drawers. A black couple came as jungle cats and looked wonderful in their costumes. The party was crowded and the music was loud. Booze was present, but we never heard any adverse comments about it. Some had too much, and that was not unusual either.

We danced all night, until time to leave, and since it was well after midnight, we spent the rest of the night with our hosts. There was no way we would be able to return to our compounds after the midnight hour had passed. We often wondered if the Saudis ever realized how their rules of conduct affected the behavior of their ex-pat workers. Hospitality in the Kingdom was out for anyone who couldn't return to their residence and needed a place to lay their weary heads.

For myself, I've never been a party person. But in this situation, you find yourself involved in everything that comes along. Why? Perhaps to taste some of life that never passed your way, maybe to see what others thought was fun, or maybe just to co-mingle with people of your own kind.

Some women went crazy with all the things available to them. We heard of British girls dancing naked on tables at a rich Saudi's palace. I have seen pictures of Saudi men leap-frogging over women at a party.

We knew some of the Filipino girls did prostitution as soon as they figured out how to get into it. An actual transaction took place before my very eyes on the streets of Riyadh, so that was confirmed and not idle gossip.

Chapter 19

The Friend Comes

After my first two years in Saudi, a longtime friend of mine came over. We had worked together for a time at the Veteran's Hospital on the same floor. Though we socialized together frequently, I had a few shady memories of our time together. There were things she'd done I wasn't supposed to know about, but secrets leaked out. I kept quiet about what I'd learned and thought of Carla as a friend. With the greatest joy, I welcomed her to Saudi and took her into our house as a room-mate.

We were invited to Dale's villa. He was an engineer who worked for Mapco, and he'd asked us for dinner and a swim. He was a very nice gentleman and a platonic friend of mine. Men are lonely in this country and having a lady to take out to eat was a pleasure for him as well as me. He never asked more of me. I enjoyed his company and he enjoyed mine. I introduced him to Carla, of course, and we enjoyed a fine evening of dining and swimming in their Olympic sized pool.

A few days after her arrival, I left Saudi to take my daughters on an extended bus tour of Europe. Two weeks later, after I'd returned, she sat in front of me and called Dale on the phone. She chatted gaily with him, without mentioning I had returned.

Warning bells rang to tell me Carla was at it again. She couldn't see me have a relationship with a man without trying to direct his attention away from me and toward her. This had happened at the hospital where we worked before.

We had primary patients. One of mine, a very ill man in his forties, became attached to me and waited for me to come to work. Seeing this, Carla went to his room frequently and flirted with him. After he recovered, he asked her out. The man had a tube for urine on his side, a urostomy. Carla didn't want to date a man with that and, in spite of all her flirting with him, she refused him.

This was whispered about on our ward. I heard about it and thought her actions very cruel. I wasn't supposed to know about it and said nothing. The man called later to ask me out, but I maintained a professional distance as we were supposed to do.

She had zeroed in on my friend Dale, the unsuspecting soul. Since I wasn't terribly involved with Dale anyway, I said nothing about it, but her treachery upset me and I didn't sleep for days. Eventually she started dating around, because Dale wasn't interested in her or in that sort of relationship.

She tried an Egyptian, whom she referred to as brown-eyes, and several others until she met Angus, the Scotsman.

From then on Carla pulled out all the stops in that relationship. He told us later she manipulated his parties so that only less attractive women were invited. She talked on the phone constantly with him and had him over to our little apartment several times.

Angus was a fine looking man who had a roving eye. He lived outside Riyadh about 60 kilometers. He had a spacious house built in the Arabian style, two stories high. It had two large sitting rooms and one large dining room, and any number of bedrooms upstairs. These homes are situated so that the men eat first and then the women enter from their sitting room to eat after the men are finished. The house also had a large, high, walled garden as well. Everything was built to ensure secrecy, and that worked for Angus, too.

Angus was an engineer, who maintained a desalinated water pumping station. His area of control contained several large pipes which poured this life giving fluid into the sprawling city of Riyadh. Angus kept the water flowing. Riyadh means garden, and the flowing waters from the Persian Gulf kept it that way.

Carla's worst offense toward Angus lay in the fact that he was married and she broke that up as well. That did not happen until he dumped her, but she caused him to be divorced. Angus had chased around on his wife for years and she no doubt knew it, but when it's thrown into your face that way, what's a woman to do? She sought a divorce. Being European, Angus no doubt ever thought of infidelity as anything worthy of note.

In time, Angus did his best to avoid Carla. He resorted to many wiles, such as telling his friend, Harry, to tell her he went to Yanbu, or Jeddah. She actually took airline flights trying to find him in some of these places, while he was at Harry's house all the while.

In one of her more desperate moments, Carla banged her head against the furniture and had bloodshot eyes for weeks after. We were privy to all the heartbreak because we were her sympathetic roommates, though she didn't know I had taken offense at her treatment of me.

Carla moved out shortly after that. Perhaps because I found it exceedingly difficult to talk to her.

About seven months after this break up. Judy and I were invited out to that station for dinner. It was not at Angus's home but at his neighbor's, Jim, another engineer. We had a great steak fry. Angus came. In fact, Jim couldn't get rid of him, though he wanted to. We didn't know what the arrangement had been made between them, but Jim had his eye on Judy, so he needed another man to join us for steak and make it a foursome.

During that evening, Angus had us over to his house to find some bit of distilling equipment for Jim to use. While there, he plied us with what he referred to as *orange surprise*. By the time we got back to his neighbor's house I felt like my head would blow off. I confess I giggled too much after that. It was orange juice, orange slices, and *sidike*, the stuff best described as pure alcohol. It was served with his soft Scottish burr which only made the *orange surprise* that much tastier and potent.

Jim became upset with Angus by that time, but that didn't faze the Scotsman at all. He sat on the floor in front of us.

"He looks like a big cat waiting to pounce!" Judy whispered to me.

Angus frequently wore all black clothes, maybe to match his black hair and eyes. It was to say the least, a very interesting evening and I did feel a bit stalked. But as he was such a handsome man, I took it was a complement.

Several weeks later we received an invitation to come out for a Christmas dinner. Judy, Nita, and I went out, this time to Angus's home. The entree turned out to be *special meat.* This is the name for pork in a country where that meat is declared illegal. We cooked a large pork roast and a full dinner. When it was time to eat, Judy lay in bed upstairs, overcome by too many orange surprises, and we ate without her. There were six or seven for dinner that night, including his neighbor, Jim.

Later, everyone drifted off to find a bed. I had a headache and searched around for something to take. Angus appeared and found some English type Tylenol for me, *Panadol*, I believe. Then he rubbed my back and asked me to his room. In those days, it didn't seem unusual at all, and I went. Maybe spending years in an unhappy marriage makes a person more susceptible to things like that. I don't know.

I do know that was the start of a long involvement that ended when he left the country and returned home. I didn't try to hide my relationship with Angus, but wondered what Carla would do if she found out about it, and she did.

At one point, I tried to date two guys at once, but had to give up a very tall Englishman. I often think about that, but it was too much for me. This was especially true when one was a Scotsman who wouldn't take no for an answer.

During our time together, a bank robbery took place. Because of that, there were roadblocks on the highway to his station continually for several months. Canny Scot that he was, he observed the times they took their breaks or changed officers. Had we gotten stopped, I would have been in the company of a male who was not a father, husband, son, or brother. For that, we both might have been sent home—or worse, to jail

Angus had it timed perfectly, and we passed over that highway many times without incident. We knew it was a risk, but we did it. I was as guilty as he, but I didn't care. Maybe I could have passed as his aunt. I was ten years his senior, though he never knew that. I didn't look it at all—being slim and in good shape helped.

For the most part we got along very well, but European people never pass up a chance to downgrade the United States. In fact it seems to be a national pastime. At one time, sitting between the Scotsman and a man from Holland, I heard continual derogatory comments about my country. Finally, I said in disgust, "I'd like you both to know, I wouldn't trade one teaspoon of Arizona sand for either one of your dinky little countries." I was really angry and added. "One half way decent atomic bomb would easily obliterate both your countries at the same time."

Maybe that's why they say those derogatory things, to cover their own inadequacies.

They laughed, but stopped their comments. Instead, the Dutchman, asked, "How old are you? You look good, have slim ankles, and a great figure."

"None of your damned business," I replied.

They just wanted to see if they could get a rise out of me, and they did. It did make me wonder—Do all older Dutch women have fat ankles and bad figures?

☙❧☙

Sometimes we had company over to visit, and I played hostess. It was a lot of fun dating this exciting man. I never really trusted him all that much, but I will always respect the toughness and wisdom of the Scots. I think it would be a rare thing if someone ever pulled the wool over that man's eyes.

He would get so excited over a bowl of course oatmeal, tears came to his eyes. Of course, in Scotland, it's called corn. Go figure. And then there was the song, "Amazing Grace." He squeezed me half to death when that played.

Finally Carla found out about the relationship and called me, crying and angry. She threatened to hurt my children, saying, "You did that to get even."

She had to know she'd hurt me to make a statement like that. She turned out to be a very vindictive person. She wrote to Angus's wife, telling her about their relationship, the meanest and biggest no-no I know of.

Angus bought me a gold necklace. One day he said, "I want to buy you something."

Judy had been talking about a Bedouin heart. I didn't know what one was, but said I'd like one. Because I am a tall woman, I chose a larger one. How did I know the thing was 22 karat gold? By the time he got a matching chain, it cost him a good bit. He paid and never said a word, but I always felt a wee bit guilty. I wore that thing everywhere, so even if he didn't want to look at it, he saw it often.

We worked twelve hour shifts which meant we had three-day weekends at least twice a month. He never took no for an answer so I spent most of those week-ends with him and some other times in between.

Another friend and I had planned a trip to Iraq to see the ruins of Babylon, but we couldn't go due to the Iraq war with Iran. I spent that week with Angus as well. I remember him saying, "You've been here for a week and I've never tired of you, not once." It made me wonder about some of his other relationships.

He and his friend from Blackpool, England, used to go over to King Fahd Hospital where the workers had little freedom. If those employees went to town, the driver of their bus took their ID badges while they went shopping. If they didn't get back on the bus, they were fired and sent home.

Angus told me they put the girls in the trunk of their car and drove out the gate with all the innocence they could muster. What a way to get girls at your party! Nothing ever got past that man, and he'd certainly be one to pull that trick.

When he had made a fresh batch of *Sidiki,* (his home brew), he hollowed out the seat back of his car and shoved bottles up there. That way he drove his potent brew through Riyadh to a party without getting caught. He did that many times without incident.

Watching him make a batch of *Sidiki* was a trip! He claimed it was easy to make, but his method was so painstaking and complicated, it took an entire week-end just for the processing. He set it to brew under a closed stairway well where there was a water heater. The warmth was perfect and after the stuff had fermented sufficiently, he set up his coils and cold water and started. He heated it, ran it through the coils, and cooled it so it dripped into containers. Then he repeated the process at least three times.

As he poured part of the brew in the toilet, I said, "You're wasting it."

He replied, "No, I am throwing away blindness, headaches, and kidney failure—the poisonous part."

I believed him and knew also if I threw a match into that commode it would have exploded into flames. No wonder the Scots make the world's finest whiskeys. They take care in what they do.

When he decided to return home, he gave plenty of notice. The Saudis were very reluctant to part with him and made his life miserable during the weeks he waited for his clearance and ticket home. They really know how to make things complicated. During the time that I had known him, this was the first time I'd seen apprehension and a touch of fear in his eyes. They had power over him and exercised it to the max. But the day finally came. He got his exit-only visa, and we parted with no few tears on my part.

Chapter 20

To The Arab's Farm

I felt an unbelievably paralyzing fear on the day the Arab said to me. "One day—someday—you come my farm." His voice, deep and heavily accented, only added to that fear. The dark glasses and hooded effect from the *gutra* and *egal,* sent a heavy, icy panic, deep inside me like nothing I've ever felt in my life. I knew him as well as could be expected since his father had been our patient over many, many months. But did I know him at all? At that moment I felt instant dread because I was a stranger in a strange land just then.

The first encounter with his family came many months before in the main hospital. The old father had had a stroke. He had been one of the main supporters of

Ibn Saud, the king who united the country and named it after his tribe, the Al Sauds. Barjas merited the utmost care and received it. He had three sons. Abdullah spoke very good English and had been to The States. The man I refer to as the Arab, spoke very little English, but wanted to, and spoke often with us to sharpen his English skills. Mohammed, the younger of them, spoke no English and was merely the younger brother as far as we were concerned.

Transferred to C-3 for that day, Barjas became my patient. Entering his room, I saw three faces set behind dark glasses and the rest of their features shrouded in the mysterious Arab *gutra* and *egal.* That in itself is daunting.

By now we understood that few Arabs even knew what good nursing care was. With help we turned our patient, which was usually done every 3 to 4 hours routinely, and gave care as needed. The men murmured, "*Shukran* sister, *shukran.*" Thank you.

They were unfailing in expressing gratitude for the care given. We found this continually as we cared for any and all of our patients.

Eventually Barjas, who basically needed long term care after the initial onset of his stroke, was transferred to MCF. Minimal Care Facility had been created to provide after-acute care to patients who could not yet go home, be it a tent in the desert or a palace.

The Arabs in no way wanted anything to do with minimal care, so the building was re-named to reflect their desire. The facility, still MCF, had been re-named Medical Care Facility. There, we cared for those with less acute conditions over longer periods of time.

The Arab then provided his father with a sitter, or *mirafic,* who lived in the room and took her meals from trays the same as the patient. He went to Pakistan to find her and interviewed several nurses before choosing Aquila from Karachi. We provided most of the care but she was always there and acted as an advocate for him as well. Thus, I had reason to feel that we knew the family, the man's mother, sisters, and other members of the family.

His older brother, Abdullah, was fluent in English. He had been to Yuma, Arizona to buy wheat especially suited for desert planting. But in spite of it all, an invitation to the Arab's farm way out in the desert, perhaps never to be seen again, sent me into breathless panic. Never in my life have I known an icy feeling like that.

"Who is there, your wife?" I asked the Arab

"I have no wife," came the answer in an ever deeper voice.

I could only stammer, "Well—er—I don't know. We are not allowed to go out like that." I shook my head in the negative, but the Arab knew so little English, who knows what he heard?

Then he said, "Not now—someday—one day—you come my farm in Azulfi."

I murmured, "We'll see."

I didn't want to seem impolite, but who knows what he had in mind? It couldn't be of a personal nature because, to him, I must have been an older woman. I quickly left the garden and returned to my duties.

We did go later, but with reinforcements. My friend, Angus wouldn't allow me to go alone into the unknown with an Arab man nor would I have considered it. This relieved my fears. Although on my own, I wasn't bound to do anything so foolish, even to satisfy my curiosity about this country. This journey was illegal in any case.

On that day, the Arab arrived at the compound in his nice Chevrolet Impala, and Angus in his station wagon. Judy, me, our head nurse, Genie, and Angus headed for the farm. As it happened, Angus had three women in his car and the Arab drove alone. Somehow that seemed unfriendly, but the Arab understood it since that was their way also—an American woman in an Arab's car. No way.

Later on, we had a tea stop. We spread out a thick, padded, Yemini blanket of wild reds, purples, and oranges to sit on while the Arab poured out sweetened tea for us. He chatted with Angus as well as he was able with his limited English and we spent a most pleasant interlude on our way to the farm. We took pictures and tried to talk.

Nearing the area, familiar monuments so often seen along roads appeared to herald the town of Azulfi. At first, we saw a huge telephone, then an elaborate Arabic coffee pot with the delicate Middle Eastern look about it with long arching spout and ornate top. Each seemed to be about ten feet high. There were others as well.

The Arab pulled up to a modest farm house. We were invited inside and seated along a wall on decorative rugs. Just in front of us, there was a fireplace used for cooking—it smoked lazily. There didn't seem to be a stove, but the fireplace had an oblong area to drag hot coals out to cook with. They served tea and dates, and we took pictures. His servant tended the fire and cleaned up.

We really didn't see much of their farming, but likely he didn't think women would be interested. He did tell us that in the early spring they planted wheat purchased from Yuma, Arizona. This wheat survived in dry areas and being springtime, they had a large crop of dark green wheat doing very well. With the moisture from spring rains, they'd get a good crop each year—if all went well, that is.

We had a tour around the town. Azulfi was an old town with crumbling mud buildings, but with newer places of business as well. The occasional camel stood tethered about. They were patient beasts and very much in use, everywhere. Then we were taken to the Arab's town house, a two-story house, grander in size and amenities. We had dinner there, sitting on the floor, of course.

We never saw a cook or servant there, but he must have had some about. The meal was a simple one, with meat and a few vegetables, accompanied by a large, round, flat Arabic bread. Fruit was served for our desert. There were few real furnishings that we saw. Maybe there were some in another part of the house. We noticed the pleasant odor of incense and spices throughout.

Azulfi is small village, far away from Riyadh and ancient. The Arab, quite prominent in the area, was an administrator of sorts. He said, "I am like sheriff—I have gun."

When his duties took him to live in Riyadh, his brother, Mohammed, took over in Azulfi, thus the position remained familial.

At bed time, he put all three of us women in his king sized bed and said to Angus, "Where you want sleep? You like sleep with me, or alone?"

The men disappeared then, but I don't believe Angus slept with the Arab.

We slept well enough and in the early morning, just after I had used the toilet—the slit in the floor type, with a cold water hose for personal cleansing—I returned to bed. Soon after, I heard the whoosh-whoosh of the Arab's long thobe as he walked about outside our door. He stopped outside it and peeked through the crack in the door. Maybe three American women in his bed might be worth looking at, even though, to an Arab we must be considered older ladies, each and every one of us.

After breakfast, he took us on a desert picnic with his friend, Abdullah. The friend had prepared camel meat stew for us and planned to cook it out there. The Arab had a Land Rover, and we went in that. We couldn't believe how hard the sand was as we drove over it without sinking. We covered huge sand dunes where there were no tracks before us. Along the way, the Arab said his father, Barjas, could find his way by tasting the sand.

Later on, we saw Arab people camping, a recreational thing they did each spring, he said. Various outfits sat far enough apart to keep the women from other campers prying eyes.

About then, the Arab began to look about for *fagah*. These are very rare and only found in the desert after spring rains. While Abdullah set out the makings of a campfire, the Arab went about looking for a rise in the sand with a crack in the center. Digging about three to four inches deep he pulled out a round mushroom-like bulb. These are about the same as truffles in Europe, and have the odor of mushroom. He said they were very expensive, about three hundred riyals per kilo.

He kept digging for the *fagah* until time to make the fire. The Arab held his robe out to stop the soft wind that blew so Abdullah could get the flames started. We thought this was to show us how they went about it out in the desert.

When the stew got going, The Arab tossed in a few *fagah* for flavor. He brushed them a bit, but didn't wash the sand off, as we found out later when it crunched against our teeth. We ate the stew and complemented our chef. It really was delicious except for the sand.

For lunch we sat in the shade of the Land Rover. Abdullah didn't speak enough English to converse, but we let him know how wonderful his stew tasted. We had tea with our lunch and the big round Arabic bread as well, a very pleasant interlude.

As the day wore on, both Abdullah and the Arab became overly interested in finding several bags of the *fagah*. Those things were a real treasure for those men, expensive, and obviously they didn't get the chance to find them every year. The Arab wanted a large bagful for his mother, and they certainly would make a fine gift for anyone knowing their value.

However, after several hours of *fagah* hunting, Angus became increasingly restless. He smiled as though really enjoying himself, but imparted this to us, "From now on, if I smile, it's a lie!" He meant it, but we were guests and our hosts believed we enjoyed this wondrous discovery as much as they did.

Nearing dark, we left the area, and how they ever found the way back, over those unmarked dunes with only starlight, remains a mystery to me. Born and raised around this area, they obviously knew the way.

We drove back to Riyadh in the same fashion as we'd come. It was too late to come into the compound, so we stayed with Angus for the night and drove in to Riyadh early the next morning.

The Arab later told me he had gotten very sleepy on the way back and said it in a tone that made me feel sorry he had to drive all that way alone. I felt guilty, but there was no help for it.

I'd helped Angus stay alert on the way back. Three hundred kilometers was a long way when tired, and we were. I couldn't help the Arab, and I felt bad about it, but it would have been very improper for one of our ladies to be seen riding alone in a car with an Arab man in his full dress costume.

Chapter 21

The Bedouin Wedding

The Saudi man who had the property in Azulfi invited us to attend a Bedouin wedding. He said his mother and sister would be there. We knew nothing of such proceedings and looked forward to the event. Angus drove Lena, our new room-mate, and me to the festivities but hadn't planned to stay.

When the Arab man saw Angus, he insisted on him attending. I believe this was an honor because this Arab held high status. He worked for a Prince of Riyadh, Sultan Salman Abulaziz Al Saud—the one who flew with our astronauts—and had charge of Bedouin affairs. Angus went into the men's side with the Arab and because he was there, we took comfort from it.

We came into a very large room, not unlike a high school gymnasium. The floor was covered wall to wall with Saudi females dressed in black and sitting on the floor. They had left pathways open to move about in. Their clothing revealed flashes of exotic fabrics beneath the somber outer wear. Most of the fabrics in the souks had large flashy borders of wild prints and gold overlays, so designed because that is all anyone ever saw. If we had wondered about the vast array of border prints, now we knew.

Everyone wore all the gold they owned, and they obviously owned a great deal of it. We saw gold worn in wide belts, vests of round, coin-like gold pieces hooked together to make a garment, along with bracelets way up the arms, and all of it eighteen carat or higher.

When a man asked a woman to marry him he must put gold on her. He may not see her face before the wedding, but he will see the bill for all the gold he must buy as well as pay for an elaborate wedding.

The Arab's mother, sisters, and nieces were there and made us very welcome. We really felt like important guests at this gathering. Everyone sat on the floor in Arab fashion. Getting up and down required a bit more agility than from a chair.

Dancing had begun, and we were invited to do our best at their style dancing. In fact, it was mandatory as far as politeness was concerned. This was no place for shyness or modesty. Lena really did a fine job of doing the very suggestive gyrations, and for myself, I did what I could, but I couldn't equal some of the energetic steps and hip wiggling we saw.

The band consisted of five black Sudanese ladies beating on drums. They sat in a circle wearing dark, non-descript print dresses covered with the *abaya*. Blue tribal tattoos marked their dark faces. Dancing was no problem with their rhythmic cadence pounding in our ears. Smoky incense drifted about and shrill, fluttering-tongued cries filled the air along with the dancing.

Frequently, someone would approach and sprinkle us with perfume, or give us a cleansing with smoking in-cense burners. Some cleansed themselves by lifting their skirts and wafting the smoke beneath. We were told the bridegroom did this beneath his dress to prepare himself for his wedding night as well.

We wondered where the bride was, and discovered later that she awaited her groom in a room above us. We never actually saw her. I don't remember seeing a table filled with wedding gifts, but I felt sure she received many of them. And if she lived in a tent, what could she have used? Where would she put them?

As the evening wore on a bit, the wide double doors were swept open and we saw Angus and the Arab looking into our area of females. This occasion called for swift lowering of facial masks and meant that supper for the women was served. The men had finished their dinner and were on their way out of the dining area so the females could go in and eat. Of course, we females ate after the men had finished.

We filed into the area where long rows of brightly printed oil-cloth had been spread out on the floor and food lay before us on platters. We found a place and sat down cross legged to eat. They have a way to eat that purportedly keeps the food safe from contamination—I think. You pick out what you want to eat with the right hand, ball it up and pop it into your mouth without touching your lips.

Never touch anything with the left hand. That one is used for personal cleanliness, if you get my meaning. Passing medication, we used the same protocol. Washing with sand wouldn't be the best in this situation, or passing meds either, but their method works—for them anyway.

A heavy-set lady dressed in black, sat across from us and kept picking out choice bits of goat for our pleasure saying, "Tah,Tah," while she urged us on with gestures.

The drinks were tea, soft drinks, or juice. The large, round, flat Arabic bread lay about at the ready to complete the meal. Tomatoes were there, too, and several varieties of fruit. When dinner ended, we returned to the women's room to continue the celebration.

Suddenly, in the midst of all the dancing, and endless chatter, the doors burst open with a loud clatter. All the Saudi ladies quickly pulled their face masks down. A group of sword bearing men started their way through all the females, escorting the very nervous bridegroom to his bride waiting up the stairs. On the way through, a few of the men grabbed handy females and swung them about amid shrieks of joy, or maybe consternation, we couldn't tell. It was a very climactic moment in this wedding celebration. Angus told me later in his lovely Scottish brogue that the groom was very excited.

After that, things wound down. We thanked our hosts and rose to our feet to find our way outside. Angus found us, and it had to be obvious to anyone that he was my companion. The Arab's sister, a very handsome widow woman in her forty's or early fifty's, whose dating or marrying years were most likely over for her, said to me, "*Shagoul es quais.*" She meant to work is good.

She took in the fine looking Scottish gentleman at my side and saw that at an older age, my life was very interesting. But that could not be so for her. I knew again that as a free-born American woman, my life was what I chose to make it. I felt bad for her then, and I still do.

Westerners often referred to a Saudi meal eaten sitting on the floor as a "goat grab." Perhaps from eating with the fingers or that the meat served usually was goat. Our Arab friend had made us honored guests of people we didn't know personally. We certainly had been treated as such.

Chapter 22

The Party Scene

Of all the party places we went, The White Elephant turned out to be the greatest disappointment. Maybe it was the general snobbishness of some English. If so, they shouldn't invite people only to ignore them. It was, however, another look-see into Riyadh night life as far as Judy and I were concerned.

One woman stands out in my mind. Tall, slender, and tanned, with long curling dark hair, she made a lovely picture for a woman in her thirties or forties. Dressed in a print sun dress, she spent the evening passionately entwined in the arms of a British man in his middle forties. We saw scenes like this repeated over and over during our time in Saudi.

Some months later, we chanced to re-visit The White Elephant. The same woman appeared. She had gained about thirty to forty pounds, was not dancing, and seemed very lonely and sad. Her man had no doubt left the country when his time was up, sadly ending a good relationship. Romances in Riyadh are fleeting and doomed to end in nearly every case. But while they last, they appear to be hot and heavy.

People we met in Saudi came from as many as twenty seven countries, with at least that many cultures or sub-cultures. Meeting and dating someone from a country your ancestors left centuries ago was a special treat. Most times you felt gratitude that your forbearers had the courage to change countries.

At Mapco one night I was asked to dance by a man I felt certain had a severe speech impediment. He made so many funny gyrations that I was suspicious of his mental status as well and didn't want to dance with him. Later I found out he was from Finland, an engineer and educated, but he spoke only Finnish. I still didn't want to dance with him, preferring the nice tall man from Manchester. That worked out well enough, but dating two men at once was more than I could handle.

One of the most memorable parties of my time in Saudi was held at the McDonald Douglas Compound. All the rooms opened onto a hallway and that area had become the dance floor. Food had been laid out in one of the rooms. Homemade and imported booze flowed freely.

We danced with everyone but the most exciting man who asked me to dance happened to be a visiting astronaut, Pete Conrad. I didn't realize it then, but he held a high administrative position with McDonnell Douglass Aircraft Corporation. He was a slight man, about my height, very pleasant to talk to, unassuming, and a very good dancer. I asked him how he came to be chosen to take a walk on the moon.

"I had the right qualifications," he answered. "And I was at the right place and right time in my life." He never played up his wonderful accomplishments, but enjoyed a night of fun and dancing under the bizarre conditions of illegality, which actually made it all more exciting.

The people at McDonnell Douglass could fly just about anything into Saudi aboard their planes since they landed on their own air strip. Just like the Royals, they brought anything they wanted, including booze or dirty calendars. No *Matawa* (religious police) would have the temerity to check royal luggage and they weren't checking astronauts either.

As far as bringing something suspect into the Kingdom, we learned that many girls merely laid dirty underwear on top of things in their luggage. The Saudis wouldn't look farther than that. They readily confiscated calendars with nude pictures or scantily clad females on them. They looked for those things diligently, especially in male luggage. More than once we saw a chagrinned man from Pakistan or India as their pictures of Hindu girls clad in scanty gold-laced costumes were taken away by Saudi inspectors.

T-shirts made for interesting reading at some of our parties. Some were downright insulting to the Saudis. At Bell Canada, a man proudly wore a shirt with four pink pigs on the front. Printed beside each pig: Sow A, Sow B, Sow C, and Sow-D. I thought to myself, *That's disgusting*! Frequently a shirt would proclaim: Happiness is an exit-only visa! It means going home and not returning.

Chapter 23

A Woman of the Desert

We received Haifa after she had spent months upon months in the main hospital ICU with severe bronchiectasis. Small, devious, and certainly very ill, this little black-eyed Bedouin woman from the Hail area stole our hearts away.

She had long been separated from her children and family life due to her severe medical condition. Because of Haifa's long term illness, her husband had readily taken another wife or two for his masculine comforts. He did, however, come to see her every few months and bring her two sons, ages about six and eight.

Haifa had left a baby girl at home, called Maha, and frequently mourned that she couldn't see her. Her husband brought the two boys to see her several times but he never brought her little daughter.

Haifa required intensive pulmonary care, relished every bit of it, and called us at every opportunity for more. She required chest percussions to loosen and bring up her thick secretions, every four hours around the clock. This consisted of being pounded on the back and chest with a thickly folded towel to cushion the blows. She loved these treatments best of all. We believed it was the physical contact, especially from male nurses, more than the clearing of her lungs. Was it the thought of a bit of forbidden touching by a male who was not a relative, or just the human touch for one so ill?

After a few months had passed, we received a percussion machine which relieved much of the work of those treatments for us. Haifa hated the loss of the human touch of our hands, especially the male hands.

At first, she refused all treatments from the machine, but as her lungs filled continually with mucus, she had to give in. It was a fight, but she came to enjoy the machine, too. Of course it was hand held, so she still had part of the human contact she craved.

Our Arab friend, acting as the liaison person for the Bedouin people in his work for the prince of Riyadh, came to see Haifa and offer his services. She happily took this opportunity to flirt outrageously, look slyly up at him, and reply to his offer of help, "You can buy me gold." He always had a bewildered look over his face when he left her room.

He really couldn't have done much for her since she would never be able to live outside of a hospital in any case, but she'd had her fun with him. In her medical state, what had she to fear from her outrageous behavior?

She grew bold in her actions where she could and, in this, took great advantage of her illness. She learned our phone numbers and many times during our hours at home, the phone would ring, usually during wakeful hours.

Answering it, I'd hear her rasping voice, "Remona— suction!" Then she'd giggle. She called Judy as well and anyone else whose number she got hold of. It was something she could do, and she did it often.

Anytime someone went on leave, she asked them to bring her something. She didn't really know what to ask for since she'd never seen a catalog to further her ideas of what we might be able to bring for her. In my case, I looked for a suitable dress, and found a *Gunny Sack* dress, a lacy feminine thing in ecru muslin, trimmed with lace, tiny round buttons, and ribbons. It had seen little wear and seemed small enough, a size five.

She delighted in it, but of course it hung on her gaunt little frame. She did love it, and later on had the joy of giving it to a female friend who visited. I realized then that to have something nice to give, equaled having something nice for one's self, and it gave her a bit of joy.

Arab customs are very generous in that way. If you ad-
mire something, you'd best not mention it or it will be
yours.

The husband brought her sons for an overnight visit.
She had a long oxygen hose attached to her tracheotomy.
With the long hose, she was able to take them into her
bathroom to bath them. She would croon to them and cry,
"Oh, my poor babies." They didn't understand her situation, but luxuriated in the soapy water as layer upon layer
of desert living washed away from their little brown bodies. This much mothering was all she had to give them.

During this time she was taken by ambulance to the
main hospital for certain respiratory treatments several
times weekly. When the orderlies loaded her into the ambulance, her sons saw her being taken away. They picked
up stones and yelled, peppering the ambulance as it
moved away.

An Arabic speaking aide explained the situation, but
it never stopped the two boys. They continued to pelt the
ambulance with rocks and fought against the hospital
staff as enemies. Their father had left them and gone back
to his desert home. He returned several days later and
took them back with him. He lived in the northern reaches of Saudi Arabia near a town called Hail.

Haifa had old, healed scars around both her wrists.
We never knew what had caused them, but stories of bru-
tality to women were frequent. We wondered if she had
been married very young, and had to be tied down for the

consummation of her marriage. This would not have been at all unusual.

Haifa spent more than three years with us at King Faisal, but the time came for her return to Hail so she would have closer contact with her family. I had to write a report on her regarding her mental and physical capabilities. The respiratory doctor, who had taken care of her for most of those three years, went along on the plane ride to tend her and see to it that she had a good situation in the northern hospital.

We thought it was above and beyond the call of duty, but we believed he wanted to see what situation she faced in the Hail Hospital. In addition, he may have wanted to see the less sophisticated health care offered in rural areas. None of us believed Haifa would live much longer in her new situation, but she would get to see her daughter Maha.

Haifa is one of the patients we would always think of and remember. Maybe being an ornery soul made her that much more of a fighter and beloved by everyone who took care of her.

Chapter 24

Holidays

Celebrating Christmas and Thanksgiving away from friends and family counted for some of our most wonderful memories. At first we spent holidays with our "family," the group we came over with and felt closest to. But as time passed we branched out to new people and new friends.

One unusual Thanksgiving dinner was spent with American women cooking for several upper-echelon British men. Add a bit of upper class to those guys and you get stilted comments such as, "Oh, Ron, I say, old chap." Their conversations, clipped and decidedly stuffy, contrasted with the regular low class blokes we'd met. All in keeping with their class, I suppose. But while it added to the interest of the day, it made me doubly glad in my heart that my ancestors saw fit to immigrate to America. I didn't even want to imagine what class structure my family once belonged to in the various countries they'd bravely left behind.

These men, doctors, department heads, and supervisors associated with no lower class men in or out of our presence. Grace, our head nurse from Florida, Jean, and some of the rest of us did the cooking, serving. These men, the same as men anywhere, were excited about tasting a Thanksgiving dinner, American or otherwise.

The dinner was interesting and delicious, but I couldn't ever remember thinking it was fun. This was because, in my heart, I knew they saw us as inferior to themselves.

We had the best time and the most fun at the Litton compound. Each unit had a large table with eight or more chairs. Someone brought over a dining set from another unit and we filled two tables with mostly Americans, Brits, Canadians, and maybe a few other countries. My friend Larry, brought us over, and he and his roommate supplied most everything. I had wonderful memories of that day. Judy and I worked hard, but many helping hands put the meal together.

How the Saudis knew to have turkeys on sale, I don't know, but they had them in all the grocery stores. They went out of their way to have something we wanted, and it was all there. They also stocked Holiday trees, too. In addition, they often outlined their buildings with electric lights at Christmas. I guess it doesn't matter what religious concept was behind this holiday as much as the excitement of it.

There was something special in celebrating a cherished holiday far from home, with no immediate family members, but with others in your same situation. It made the meaning of the day much dearer and more comforting to us and, perhaps, everyone. In the background, music played while everyone laughed and talked and, later, the *sidike* flowed steadily as well.

Sometimes the celebrating got fast and furious because it was so illegal, so intense, and so far, far, from everything familiar. It was with bittersweet emotions I remembered these events. One Thanksgiving, I was invited along with Dan, my British friend, at eat on the Air base.

At this all American meal, Dan enjoyed the excess with which we Americans celebrate Thanksgiving. It had been held on the military base where Alida's officer was stationed. The table held twenty people and every seat held a participant. Alida, as our hostess, served turkey, stuffing, mashed potatoes, cranberries, and much, much more. They also had real booze, including Johnny Walker Red, which doubly impressed Dan.

Later, we enjoyed the British version which was held at the home of Dan's friend. Their potatoes were not so fattening, being thick sliced, seasoned, and roasted in the oven. It was a lovely meal, as well. I hadn't realized the British celebrated Thanksgiving, though most civilizations would, of course, have cause to celebrate a good harvest.

Chapter 25

Alya

There are many tragic stories to be told of those we came in contact with in the Kingdom of Saudi Arabia. Many of them had to do with ancient custom, cruelty, or simple ignorance of a better way. Since any sort of world-wide education of the Bedouin appeared to be absent during our time in Saudi, we saw many tragedies first hand. Not that they were the only part of the population so afflicted. At that time, lack of medical knowledge existed among the wealthy or even the royals who were well educated.

Alya was born to a Bedouin couple living in the northeastern area near a town called Hofuf (ho-foof). They already had two or three children lying beneath the desert sands, and we hadn't been told the reason for these deaths. The doctors in Hofuf sent this newborn to King Faisal Hospital and Research Centre soon after her birth.

Alya had a birth defect that made it impossible for her to eat, suck, or breathe normally. Her tongue and surrounding tissues were nearly adult sized which occluded those passages. This was a birth defect of unknown cause, though the Saudi custom of marrying cousins frequently results in defects, including defective heart valves, strabismus, mental deficiencies, and others.

When we received this child at MCF, she had been the recipient of tender loving care by Western personal for about two years. At first she took her food via a tiny feeding tube until she had grown enough to allow her to eat. Even now she was fed with great caution on the part of the staff to prevent choking and inhaling food. She had begun to eat solid food, mouth words, and spoke more English than Arabic when she came to us.

She easily made herself and her needs known and had developed a lively and trusting attitude toward staff and everyone she came in contact with. Through the years in the hospital she had been gifted with tiny gold earrings, solid gold bracelets, many nice dresses, and a very fine pair of red leather French shoes. She was a Saudi female of worth, totally comfortable with herself, and treated that way by everyone.

She had a mop of thick curly hair, black snapping eyes, and though her mouth protruded with the very large tongue, she had no awareness of her deformity. The doctors at Faisal knew that any kind of surgery would be needless butchery. They said that in time her protruding tongue would fit well enough in an adult mouth. She might never be a great beauty, but with the mask, it wouldn't be known to anyone other than family members.

Alya developed friendships quickly among our staff and her former nurses came often to visit her. This softened the pain of the sudden change in her life. She roamed about the ward and accompanied us on our rounds with the med cart.

She took a special interest in Hassan, a handsome, curly headed, dark-skinned Sudanese young man who had hopes of becoming a doctor in the future. She often followed him about, played peek-a-boo with him, and called out frequently, "Hathan, Hathan." Then giggling, she happily ran from him, only to return and hang on his leg as he worked.

She grew bigger and continually received new clothes and gifts from us and from her former care givers. As she grew her tumor stayed the same size giving us hope the doctors were on the right track with her care. She ruled the roost on our ward and became a constant delight to all. Like any child, she resisted going to bed.

We asked Mohammad Waddidi to put Alya to bed one evening. When he came out of her room, we asked, "Did you put Alya to bed?"

He held out his hands in futility. "No—she refuses."

We did not press him because no male from another country dared to force a Saudi female to do anything. Not even in this case, where she was a patient and he, a care giver. Waddidi, a fine, gentle man with a family of his own in the Sudan, knew very well that any infraction of the rules in the treatment of Saudi women meant immediate dismissal.

Perhaps he remembered what happened to Yussef, a good man who was fired and sent home over an incident. Yussef had been assigned to take vital signs. When putting a blood pressure cuff around a Saudi woman's arm, she complained that his hand had touched her breast. He denied it, but it may have happened since the hand in wrapping the cuff might accidentally have brushed against her body. I know mine certainly has many times.

They discharged Yussef from his hospital job and deported him back to Somalia in disgrace. We thought him a wonderful young man and believed him innocent, but the woman, a Saudi female, in this case had to be believed. From that time on we allowed no male to enter that female patient's room except her doctor. Not even the Egyptian food servers with their outrageously rank body odor were allowed in her room. We didn't want another such incident and truly believed the woman to be rather vindictive.

We believed causing trouble for others was one outlet for entertainment in their cloistered lives. I had that thought many, many times from incidents I observed. Household gossip, comparing children and clothing, and snipping at other females might be all the entertainment they had.

As time went on, the powers that be decided Alya should get to know her parents. Basically strangers to this pampered little miss, they were brought in from the desert from time to time to visit her. These people had the outdoorsy look of the desert dweller, and it seemed to me, some suspicion of us. Their clothing bore the odors of campfire smoke, and they appeared poor indeed.

They came and stayed in her room for about two weeks, interacting and playing with their daughter. This visit was to get used to her and for her adjustment to them, as well. The day came for her discharge and Alya went home to her tent in the desert near Hufuf. As a group we worried about her future but the time for her to return home had come.

We heard nothing more for at least a year. Then one day, the parents brought Alya back to King Faisal hospital. The nurses told us she had become a quivering, pitiful mass of traumatized child. She was returned to the ICU ward where she had been so carefully nurtured for the first two years of her life. The nurses who had cared for her previously cried bitter tears at the sight of this pathetic, silent child.

Gone now was the outgoing, trusting little girl who flirted with Hassan and chased him about the ward. Alya was instead, a pitiful, cringing, little creature who shrunk away from anyone who came near. As the story unfolded, it seemed her parents were not inclined to wait for time to correct Alya's swollen tongue. They sought the advice of a doctor near them in Hofuf.

Of Indian decent, he was proud of what his education, and the medical prowess his country had to offer. He advised they send their daughter to India for corrective surgery. The very word *docteur* embodies wisdom and skill beyond the imaginings of the unlettered Bedouin, and they followed the advice given.

Of course the results were disastrous, and the parents returned her to Faisal, hoping they could restore her once again. The hospital staff did their best, but the damage had been done and Alya no longer ate food normally or talked, but cringed in her crib like the wounded creature she had become.

Abnormality is not looked upon favorably by many, but in Saudi Arabia, if a female isn't marriageable, her worth is greatly diminished. Patience is not one of their virtues and they chose not to wait for nature to help their child toward normalcy. Perhaps other members of their tribe were disturbed by her appearance. We'll never know why they sought further medical intervention, nor will we ever know what eventually became of Alya. We do know we will never forget that poor little child who suffered so greatly because of ignorance and superstition.

Chapter 26

Jack and Jill

Jack was handsome, charming, and oh, so interested in the woman he happened to meet at one of the many, many parties around Riyadh. Jill attended this party with a friend, Mary, who knew the people and frequented their activities. The men quickly evidenced their preference for Jill over her less attractive friend Mary. And this caused hard feelings between the two women.

Jack made certain to take Jill's phone number but not Mary's, which created another disturbing wedge between them. A handsome man will win out in any case, and he came to take Jill to his compound for several visits whenever he could borrow a vehicle. Cool and cagey, he underplayed his hand. But as time passed, tension mounted until they erupted into a very passionate union.

They crashed into furniture, glass was broken, furnishings scattered, and one of them suffered an injured back. Nothing stopped them during this passionate, all-consuming sexual union.

Jill was entranced by his British slant on things, American, or otherwise—and certainly his fine Clint Eastwood looks—and stayed too long in that alliance. It was to become an ego damaging as well as a physically damaging alliance.

Jack was taken by her handsome features and friendly, open, happy go lucky ways. Unfortunately, this made her an easy target for his devious sociopathic nature. They became one of the many ex-pat couples dating, dancing, partying, and doing all things illegal in the Kingdom.

In the compound where Jill lived, a male guest was allowed only fifteen minutes before he had to exit the gate. This time allotment, monitored by guards at the gate, and no doubt jealous of our liberties, was closely kept.

A little thing like that proved no deterrent to Jack. Upon one trip when returning Jill to her housing, and finding no one else at home, he devilishly challenged Jill. "Come on, we can do it." And laughing so hard they barely made it up the stairs to the bedroom, they completed their mission. Then he drove innocently out the gate, a wide smile across his lips.

On another occasion, Jack scaled the eight foot walls surrounding the compound and spent the night. In the morning, he sauntered without challenge out the gate with so many others on their way to work. We never found it difficult to manage these sorts of things since we pretty much all looked alike to the guards. We were *infidels* working in the Kingdom and taking the Kingdom's oil money.

Some Saudis never thought of the sacrifice we made in leaving our own country to provide them with the wonders of modern medicine. Many times we were met with accusations of taking away the Kingdom's money. Some thought we used their oil while leaving ours in the ground. Yet if we didn't buy it, where would their wild spending sprees come from?

Jack soon found a huge American car and became the proud owner of a Cadillac. This was a car only dreamed of in his own country of narrow roads and pricey petrol. How he delighted in the luxury of tooling about Riyadh in that huge boat of a car. Gas cost about twenty five cents per gallon in the Kingdom.

Road construction about the streets of Riyadh may or may not be cordoned off with warning signs. Near the Al Azizia Market, referred by us as the A & P, some sort of road construction was in progress. Passing through that area earlier, all seemed well. Later, after dark, Jack and

Jill returned from shopping at the Glass Mall. Jill suddenly realized they were headed straight into a huge, deep, hole in the road with nary a barrier in sight.

Jill screamed a warning, but as the words escaped her lips, the car plunged deep into an excavation that easily held the entire Cadillac. Returning to consciousness, after the initial shock, Jack realized he had to get Jill out of the entire scenario and away. If not, they would both face deportation or jail, should they be found together.

Rousing Jill from her coma-like shock, he pushed and shoved her out to the top of the excavation and sent her stumbling toward the Al Azizia Market. Just as she disappeared from the scene, the police arrived.

Someone had seen Jill and informed the police. They took far more interest in finding the "madam" who had been seen in the car than in the accident itself or Jack's state of health.

They asked, "Where madam?"

Jack said, "There is no madam."

"Where madam?"

Again Jack denied the presence of a woman.

Unbelieving, they searched the area but found no female in the immediate area who appeared to have been involved in the accident. They completed their investigation, though perhaps not to their satisfaction, and allowed Jack to leave the scene to find his own way home. His lovely big auto was now totaled.

At the market, Jill slowly worked her way through the isles purchasing a few items of food. As always, she took a ride to the compound on the bus as if she had been on a shopping trip all the while. We all used this ploy when going and coming from the various compounds we visited. Her pale, bruised face and limping movements were seemingly not noticed.

❧❧❧

When meeting a date for a weekend or night out, we would take a ride on the shopping bus to a market. Several markets provided this service. We usually carried a small bag, bulging with overnight necessities. After arriving at the market we got into our date's car and left for a night, a weekend, or even a week.

The return trip home might be in hours or days, but during most day and evening hours, those shopping busses ferried passengers for groceries. Since women were not allowed to drive, it helped us in getting our food supplies. Everyone used the busses this way and no one ever complained, certainly not any of the drivers or the guard on the gate.

We were very lucky at Faisal since they never took our ID badges if we got off one of the hospital conveyances. We knew this was not the case at other hospitals. For those workers, if they didn't return, and the driver held their ID badge, they became a fugitive from the law.

If caught, and if they were lucky, instead of jail, they would be sent home.

Jill went to work the next morning saying she had bumped into a drawer to explain her bruised facial areas. Jack returned to his practice of borrowing an old truck when he could get hold of it.

As time went on, his controlling nature caused friction between them, and their ardor began to cool. At gatherings or parties Jack watched her every move and became angry if another man paid her attention. With her fine appearance, men constantly approached her. She danced with them as well as socialized. Because of this, and the multitude of real differences that all people have, they frequently fought, but made up later on.

In time, Jack's contract in the Kingdom ended, and he returned to England. He kept in contact and Jill often flew to London to meet him. He proposed marriage, and against her better judgment, she accepted. Jack had been a married man when they met, but he had told Jill that he had divorced his wife.

On one of Jill's trips to London, she married the man and began procedures to bring him to The States. Jill's contract neared the end, and Jack went to The States to secure employment in her home town and await her return home. She wrote many of her friends in the Northwest to ask their help in getting her husband situated. They happily helped Jack find a place to live and employment as well.

The end of the story is not as exciting or romantic as the beginning. Jill returned home to find she had married a cruel, conniving, controlling, sociopath who had used her to get a green card. Life with him quickly became intolerable and the alliance dissolved like the thin air it was founded upon. But not before her health, her heart, and her finances, including all her Saudi gold, lay sold, broken and decimated. Jack had not one wife stashed around the world, but several.

He had never divorced any of them, nor did he offer support to his various and sundry offspring. A handsome face with a foreign accent didn't look quite so exciting after hearing about this unfortunate girl's affair.

Chapter 27

Two Little Girls

Our ward received those patients in need of recuperation or terminal care as the case required. At nearly the same time, we received Ameera, a fourteen-year-old girl afflicted with Lupus Erythematosis, and Hamda, a twelve-year-old, with the same disease. This was an auto-immune disease that more frequently afflicted young women, but can occasionally affect males as well.

Hamda was a petite, beautiful child who bore the marks of the severely ill. Her little face, was constantly flushed with fever, her slim body twisted in misery as her immune system worked against her own body tissues to destroy her. We kept her in as much comfort as possible and treated her condition with all that medical science had to give for this difficult, chronic, condition.

Ameera had obviously been ill for a long time before her family sought medical attention, and she had regressed into an animal-like state. She kept her bedding twisted, wet, and stained with feces and urine. Her wild tangled hair and snarling utterances presented a fearsome picture to the nursing staff. She no longer spoke, but moaned, cried, snarled, and spat. We kept the floor covered with plastic sheeting to save the carpeting and cut down on housekeeping.

As time went on Hamda gradually regressed into death as Ameera slowly responded to treatment. The nurses and Arabic-speaking staff worked daily to reclaim Ameera from her animal-like state. Over time, she began to speak a few words and to relish being clean and properly dressed. Toilet training progressed to the point where she was once again continent. The staff taught her to walk once again, and her stiffened, contracted legs, slowly took on new strength.

After frequent scolding by the Arab speakers, Ameera stopped spitting over the side of her bed onto the floor, although more than one girl from the desert spit freely over the rails and thought nothing of that behavior. I came to believe that in their home situation, sputum sinks into the desert sands and is purified by the fierce, burning sun.

The day came when we turned Hamda towards Mecca, and she passed away. The saddened staff continued on with Ameera. It took many weeks, but she slowly changed from the wild, animal-like child into a young woman. As she progressed, her menses returned. They had ceased during the height of her illness or had never begun.

Ameera's mother visited often. Upon discovering her daughter's menses had returned, she quickly put a Bedouin mask on the girl. No longer was this young woman's face to be seen by any male not closely related to her. Her condition had changed from being seriously ill to that of a young female in stable condition. In any case, she would always have Lupus. It could be controlled in some cases, but not really cured.

Not long after, we saw that the mother and father arranged for an interview regarding possible marriage for Ameera. At fourteen, she might have been a bit past the age for marriage in some circles. But with a long and chronic illness, she could not have been in the market for a husband. That part of her history we never knew.

A man, dressed in traditional clothing, was brought in to see her. Masked and nicely dressed, she may have passed inspection. We weren't sure. Unsettled and upset about this, we went to Abdullah, an educated man whose father was our patient. We asked him about this situation. We did not mention her name, but told him about her case and that she was now under consideration for marriage.

"She will be one of his wives, the third or fourth," he replied. "He may be a relative of hers. In this case, she will have a home to live in, the status of being a wife, and will be cared for in that way."

We considered his reply and realized that this would be a better way for her than living at home in an unmarried state, especially with other marriageable sisters. Being considered eligible for marriage in spite of a chronic condition would enhance her sense of worth. If she was able to have a male child, she would have done all her culture asked of a Saudi female.

How often we wonder what ultimately became of so many of our female patients that lingered in our memories.

Chapter 28

My Amaliya

My feet became painful, not too much, but enough to ask a doctor about the repair of bunions that made my feet unattractive. I hated how they stuck out of sandal straps, reminding me of my mother's malformed feet. I went to the doctor complaining of pain in my feet.

He said I should have corrective surgery. It cost me nothing and I would have the first month off work at full pay. After checking around, I knew which doctors to ask to perform the surgery. I asked Dr. Lifeso of Canada, a most highly recommended orthopedic surgeon to do my surgery and Dr. Robinson of England to pass the gas (handle the anesthesia. They agreed to do the surgery and

Dr. Lifeso, after checking the x-rays, said to me, "I won't have to break any bones."

I became a patient and had the surgery. I knew I wouldn't ever take Ativan again because it caused amnesia for me. Awake and chatting in recovery, I had no recollection of any of it and regretted the loss of a small part of my life.

Awake, I saw my bandaged great toes were pulled away from my other toes and looked like a thumb. I heard the doctor say, "I broke a bone in each foot." Too befuddled to know how to think about his statement, I only knew the surgery was over.

During my time in the hospital, the Arab and the sitter for his father, the Pakistani woman, Aquila, came to see me and brought flowers. I still have his card, written: *congratulato for you Remondo.* I will always be very touched by his efforts at writing the card in English.

Another friend, Larry, brought in a snort of *Sidki,* which I didn't drink, and tried to entertain me with a game or two, but I couldn't concentrate.

Judy did her best at helping me make sense of things by saying such gentle words as: "Why don't you wake up, you dip-shit?"

Medicine and I weren't a good mix, but her touch of reality helped a lot.

At home, I crawled around. Walking was awkward and painful, but I could if I had to. Coffee, so very important in my life, became difficult since I couldn't hobble with a cup of coffee. I found crawling and scooting the cup on ahead did the best for me though my knees got a work out.

I spent most of the time on the couch with my feet elevated, watching TV or reading Wilbur Smith books. The television came on at noon and had two English speaking channels. One was hospital English with Arabic lessons and Arab news in English for the Arab speaking impaired. The other English Channel played Riyadh English. On that one we got the local news and occasionally some world news. The local news usually consisted of the royals kissing each other's cheeks as they greeted a dignitary from a visiting country.

They often played American or English TV programs after carefully editing them for salacious content. Dallas and Dynasty came on, but never in sequence so we never knew if Jock Ewing would be alive or dead, and Ellie with the new or old husband. Best of all, we saw many British humor shows. Those were very funny. We became enamored of British humor, and still are. Their humor was frequently raunchy, but always hilarious.

Trying to pass the time wasn't designed for sanity, but there were a few interruptions. On one of my visits to the doctor, I met a patient who was visibly upset at seeing one of their nurses in a wheel chair.

This man was a former patient of ours afflicted with throat cancer. In spite of buttons to hold in his trach and a raging illness, I believed this man, Ahmed Shamlah, a

Yemeni man, to be about the handsomest man I had ever seen in my life. He put the likes of Errol Flynn or George Clooney to shame. I could not describe him, but his face lingers in my mind because of his incredible masculine beauty. He smiled broadly to see one of his former nurses, but remained silent, unable to ever speak again. He must have been in for a check-up at the outpatient clinic.

I felt the warmth of caring in his look. I explained I had had an *amyliah* pointing to my bandaged feet. This made me feel closer to the Arab people because of their obvious concern.

I have come to believe that the little people of any country are usually decent hard working souls who want peace and stability to raise their families in their own time honored traditions. It's the people who hold the reins of power we need to be wary of, as they all too often have other agendas.

Staying home for a month in our small apartment drove me rat-traps until one day Aguila, the Pakistani woman who was a *mirafic* for the Arab's father, came to my house with a wheel chair. She took me to the MCF to visit my patients. I cannot forget the look on Salem's face when he saw me in the wheel chair, upset that I might share his condition which was paraplegia from an auto accident.

Trying to reassure him that I had had an *amaliya,* or surgery, and would walk again, my Arabic was not good enough. I carefully covered my feet around the Arabs, but

I managed to get up and walk a few steps for him. I had already learned a very harsh lesson regarding that.

I didn't know that displaying the soles of your feet to anyone is the grossest of insulting behaviors. I nearly went to prison for it, and my friend, Larry, along with me.

Early in my recovery period, Larry came to take me to the bank, located in the basement of the hospital. He came to the door and I hobbled to the car. I had a wheel chair and at the hospital, he rolled me down the long, long, corridor to the bank. I found this embarrassing and asked him how he could stand to roll me around in a wheel chair with my bandaged feet sticking out. His reply was the best thing I'd ever heard, and I would never forget.

Being a man of few words anyway, he said, "Because you're good looking, you laugh a lot, and you're built like a brick shit-house."

I said nothing, because I didn't know what to say, but it gave me a soft warm glow inside to hear that from him, or any man for that matter. He kept on wheeling me down the hall and we never mentioned it again, but he knew I heard him.

Later as we wheeled about the streets of Riyadh, my feet, so used to being elevated, began to swell and hurt severely. For relief, I put them up in the car window and oh, it felt so good!

We noticed a police car following us but not believing the police were interested in us, we leisurely drove about until the cop put his flashing lights on. Being near, we drove into the parking lot of my compound and stopped.

The officer, a Saudi, came to the passenger side. I opened my window.

White faced, and shaking with fury, he rattled off his complaints in rapid fire Arabic, and gestured at my feet. As I lowered them to the floor, I pointed to the heavy bandages and tried to tell him in my best hackneyed Arabic. "*Ana amaliya in Mustashfa.*" Grimacing, I added, "*Fee alum kateer.*" With my best gesturing and halting speech, I explained I had had surgery at the hospital and had a lot of pain. I pointed to the (*gasseria*), wheel chair, in the back seat.

He didn't buy it and turned his attention to my friend, Larry. We were no relation to each other, another big offense, and panic at our situation ran rampant. I still did not realize our biggest offense was my feet displayed in the window. And Larry would, of course, be at fault, not being able to control his woman.

Then, thank God, the Saudi guard came out of the gate house and pointed to a large black limo sitting there. Apparently some important official was lurking around and the guard didn't want any trouble at that time. He, in effect, told the policeman to get lost and threatened him with this official if he didn't.

So due some kind of pomp and circumstance we never understood, we were spared the untold horrors of a Saudi jail, probable infection of my surgical wounds, and for sure, deportation. For Larry, an important man with his company, he faced the loss of a wonderful job with nice living quarters, and in addition, the horrors of a male Saudi jail.

How did we know about a Saudi jail? We were told by a Scottish man who had been involved in an auto accident. Assumed guilty, until proven innocent, as was their legal process, he was tossed into a male Saudi facility. The man had suffered a fracture of one of his leg bones, and painful rib injuries. No medical attention was offered to him in that jail.

He found himself in amongst many unwashed men similarly ensconced, sitting on a befouled cement floor. The toilet facilities, a hole in the floor somewhere in the room, sufficed for them all.

He didn't say if it had a water hose nearby. After three days of agony, he had a visitor. It took him thirty minutes or more to drag himself over to the screen where he could speak with his visitor.

Later then, he was transferred to their equivalent of our county hospital, that horror of a hospital, Shemaze. We often sent patients over there and knew what the care there was by both report and by hands on viewing.

Once there, the Scotsman received some sort of care for his condition and ended his story by saying, "The jail was f---ing better than that bloody hospital!"

So, in reflecting back on the incident, we knew we had been saved by a fluke. I learned the hard way that you don't show the soles of your feet to anyone unless you want to insult them in the worst possible way.

I guess they forgot to mention that in our orientation. For that reason, I carefully kept my feet covered as best I could upon my visit to see my patients, and I visited my patients several times during my month off. And when the time came to return to work, I was glad to go.

Larry took me to his compound several times. It had the furnishings of a modern American style home. They told us that when it was in the planning stage an American housewife had been consulted. Her designs made that home into a very convenient place to be.

We watched *The Thornbirds* and ate wonderful food. He had a great kitchen and Judy made many a great meal in it. We were treated as honored guests and spent many happy hours there. Working away in the kitchen, Judy casually mentioned to the guys, "You know, Ramona's afraid of the garbage disposal."

I don't know what made her say that, but we laugh about it still.

I returned to duty wearing sandals tied on with bandages. I had an eight-hour day which seemed an eternity, but despite wanting to lie on the floor with my feet propped up on the wall, the day passed. After another three day week-end, the twelve hour shifts began. Each day became better, but feet are slow to heal. Normal shoes were impossible for nearly two years, but I like my feet now.

Chapter 29

Our People in Saudi

We worked with a woman who spent her time in ways that brought shame on our country, our religion, and our profession as well. Lorna—we called her the teacher—was a woman in her forties. She was large boned and a bit overweight with thick, gray-streaked, blonde hair. Her nursing skills were adequate, but her sexual skills must have been something to write home about.

We had two three-day weekends each month and Lorna spent them in Dhahran with a young Saudi man, teaching him the finer points of sexual congress. She laughed about her trips and flashed huge rolls of 100 Riyal bills. The man paid for her airfare and her services each time.

This went on for months until we wondered what else she could possible teach the man. She also did a bit of tutoring on the side, since we often saw her taking rides from men on the street. We thought her activities extremely foolish, but it wasn't our place to teach the teacher rules of safe behavior on the streets of Riyadh.

One night, Judy and I returned from a dinner at the Intercontinental Hotel. Our escorts dropped us off that evening about nine. As our friends drove away, we saw a figure weaving and limping her way up the sidewalk toward our compound. Not wanting her to know we had seen her this way, we walked down the street a little distance to keep an eye on her and wait where we wouldn't be seen. After several minutes, we watched Lorna limp slowly through the gate and down the street toward her apartment. We waited a while longer then sauntered casually through the gate as though we had just arrived. The guard, a Saudi, seemed very agitated and questioned us about the woman.

His black eyes glittered with distaste as he asked repeatedly, "Who is madam?" he demanded. "You know madam—where she live?"

We shrugged, denied knowing anyone like that, and left. Leaving the gate area, we watched from the shadows to make sure Lorna got to her quarters. We couldn't miss her torn and disheveled state. Her hair was matted with grass and sticks, her face was swollen and bruised, and her nose dripped blood.

She made it to her door, managed to open it, and staggered inside. We returned to our own quarters, shaken and worried for Lorna. We knew she'd survived a rough encounter with one or more of the strange men she'd picked up on the street. Men she didn't know, but who saw her as a prostitute of the lowest order.

The next morning, on the day shift, Lorna called in. She said she had lost the key to the pool area and tried to climb over the fence and fell. The doctor x-rayed her and found she had a couple of broken ribs. She missed a few days of work. She never bragged about her trips to Dhahran after that.

Things like that made Western women look like prostitutes. That was what they thought we were and behavior like that only bolstered their opinion of it. We also resented the damage to our reputations. Our nursing skills usually left a good impression on the people and they readily expressed their appreciation for the care we gave them. But that we were Infidels to them remained in their minds as well.

One Saudi man told a friend of ours that he had refused to allow his daughter to enter the nursing profession. After seeing the skills we possessed and the real help the profession could offer the Saudi people, he relented.

People like Lorna cast a black cloud over the good and caring expertise we brought to the people. She wasn't the only one who did these things. Where there was money to be made, there would be those who would do what they must to get some of it.

Another woman, who should never have been hired, left a different impression. Connie had had a severe illness that took her to death's door prior to her hire. Few people have ever contracted botulism and lived, but Connie had. Her friend, who ate the same contaminated tuna, died.

Connie had received specific treatment for each of the deadly symptoms of botulism as they occurred, and after months of tubes and respirators, she recovered. A thing like that weakens the body and spirit for years to come, and we felt this had been the case with her. We had already come to realize just how strong someone has to be, to survive emotionally living in a strange and sometimes hostile environment.

A few months after her appearance in the Kingdom, Connie's innate weakness caught up with her. She worked at the Medical Care Facility with us, but on a different floor. On Connie's ward, the patients were given all the medications that would normally be sent home with them. Thus, numerous patients had bags of medications in their possession, Morphine, Demerol, Valium, Seconal, antibiotics, and a host of others for sleep, pain, and infection in pill form and readily available to anyone.

They kept these medicines under their beds. Few of the patients ever realized the quality of narcotics in their possession.

Things like that did not happen in American hospitals or extended care facilities because medications of this kind were locked up until the patient was discharged. The native people didn't like relinquishing their personal belongings, even if ordered by the *doctuer*, thus the presence of many tempting drugs for the taking.

One day Connie did not come to work as scheduled, and on the phone sounded extremely drowsy. Found to be heavily sedated, she was hospitalized for narcotics overdose. The Saudi police had to be informed. Enraged at this flouting of Saudi law against the use of drugs, they demanded her arrest immediately.

Her doctor was able to refuse them and would not release her to the police. He kept on refusing for several months claiming she was too ill. It was not her physical state so much as her mental state. Connie's life in a Saudi women's prison would have meant her death and he knew it.

For months, Connie had around the clock nurses sitting with her, more to show the Police her serious state of health than actually required. She became pale and emaciated from her hospital stay. She was very afraid of what would happen to her. Nurses wept for her shame and agony and Judy was one of them.

This poor nurse had a close escape and a fight to the end on the part of her doctor. Connie trembled in fear each hour of her incarceration until the day finally came. Her doctor had succeeded in getting her on a plane to the U. S. and safely home.

That doctor had waged a heroic fight on her behalf. The Saudi Police believed she had committed an evil crime in their Kingdom. Being a female, any claim of extenuating circumstances in her defense meant nothing. Being female only made her offense doubly a crime.

I had a few run-ins with British nurses while working there. One in particular was a pretty, young blonde woman. Amanda, being British, felt she'd hung the moon. We staffed the Lithotripsy floor at that time and our patients went over to the main hospital for the treatments that pulverized renal stones by ultrasonic sound waves. On their return, they were treated as post-surgical patients, which is what they were.

When Saleh returned from his procedure, I asked Amanda, a nurse II, which is equal to L.P.N. in The States, to do his post-op vitals.

"In England we don't bother to do them for this procedure," she replied, her nose in the air. "But if you want them done, you can jolly well do them yourself." She sniffed her disdain and walked off.

This patient had undergone anesthesia, had his kidney region subjected to intense sonic waves that broke apart his renal calculi, and had bloody urine draining from his catheter from super hydration and bits of stone passing painfully through his ureter and urethra. A ureter is the tube from the kidney to the bladder.

Of course I reported her behavior. I was asked by the supervisor to write a report on this particular nurse since she was up for re-hire and they didn't want her back for many other infractions as well.

This nurse along with Lorna, the one we called the teacher, often let Saudi men into the stair well of the facility in the darkness of the night shift. It wasn't seen by us, but we heard they entertained them in their usual fashion. We could only surmise what they offered but what we did see was the two of them bringing their Arab gentlemen into our break room for refreshments. This is such a no-no, and totally against the rules.

I did include what we actually saw in my report and the girl was not re-hired. These things committed by uncaring souls sullied the reputations of all Western women in the eyes of the Saudis.

We did hear also that Amanda frequently danced naked on a table or two at some of the palaces around Riyadh. Of these feats, she bragged repeatedly. She would laugh about it while jiggling the gold bracelets she wore around her soft, white, wrists, and shaking her luscious blonde hair. Another English girl took a massage tour around the world, stopping off at all the major cities on the way.

One of the choicest events that happened involved an American woman who liked to toss big names about in her conversations. Donna Larson inferred she was related to Joe Namath, the big name athlete, and knew him intimately. She claimed as bosom buddies Chuck and Di, of English royalty, and any other person of worldwide interest at the time.

She sounded completely knowledgeable about everything happening around Riyadh. She constantly received bouquets of cut flowers on the wards from her devoted husband, a military officer at one of the stations in Riyadh. Oh how the woman bragged about her accomplishments and friends!

She constantly followed people into rooms to observe procedures being done, inserting an IV, putting down a naso-gastric tube, dressing a wound, or even passing medications. It gave us the feeling she might be inspecting our work though we knew she didn't have the rank for that.

We took all the bragging and name dropping in stride and, in due time, they promoted Donna to head nurse of one of the floors at MCF. As she was selected over more senior nurses, this caused some hard feelings.

A month or two later, lo and behold, the woman had been found out. She held no nursing degree and no license to practice. She was not married either. Now we knew why she followed us into the rooms. She needed to see how things were done, and those lovely cut flowers she received were sent by herself.

Along about this time, we were treated to some real name dropping. Judy came home from work in high spirits. She exclaimed, "Guess who I took care of today?"

I couldn't, but she laughed, saying, "I had Mohammed Ali for my patient today. He came for the Hajj and decided to visit Faisal for a check-up."

She told us all about her exciting day. "He was so nice!" she added. "He posed for pictures with me for my sons, signed autographs for everyone, laughed, and joked all day with the staff." Judy didn't mention his state of health as that would be a private matter at any rate. "He's a really big man and about the friendliest patient I've ever had," she said with a smile.

Sometimes we had invitations to compounds outside of Riyadh. In this case, another friend, Dolly, and I were invited to the Saudia Compound in Jedda. I had never been there and hadn't seen the Red Sea, either, so we were interested.

When we arrived, our hosts picked us up and drove us to their compound. Our hosts were men who kept the Saudia planes "churnin' and burnin'." We were informed of this by a very inebriated aircraft mechanic in his best slurring voice. I hid my shock at the idea of a drunken mechanic maintaining aircraft, but there hadn't been any recent crashes, so I passed it out of my mind. Our host quickly gave each of us long dresses to wear, as Dolly's extra short skirt nearly caused him to pass out when he picked us up at the airport.

They fixed wonderful steak dinners for us and took us driving around town. Jeddah has a drive along the shores of The Red Sea called the Cornish. Along it are many tall monuments depicting: fifty-foot-high sheaves of wheat, a beautiful Arab horse head monument, three full-sized ships, a tower of balls with a crescent on top, six very tall spears, a group of lined blue towers, and several finely done rounds depicting seascapes, and some we couldn't decide upon, but it certainly made for a wonderful drive along the sea front.

We noticed many people wore western wear, and we saw far fewer *thobes* and *gutras* in evidence. Women, of course, were masked, but overall, the religious fervor seemed a lot less in Jeddah.

It was hot and very muggy along the Red Sea coast. The next day, we drove to a place where we could swim unobserved. On the way, we decided to drive the highway leading to the holy city of Mecca. We reached the point where the road forked. Muslims could enter the city of Mecca, non-Muslims could not. A road to circumvent Mecca had been provided for non-Muslims who were traveling in that direction. We turned back toward the Red Sea, but we had seen the spot where the faiths were separated.

At the Red Sea, we prepared to snorkel and see all the wonderful sea creatures and reefs so famous worldwide. It was windy and a shallow half-mile out to the area we sought. We tried to get over sharp coral and struggled against choppy, rising waves. After fighting my way from shore through waves and the coral, I decided I didn't want to drown trying to walk on swim fins over the uneven, biting, coral outcroppings. After I called out, "Help" a time or two, I realized I was on my own and began to struggle my way back. On dry sand at last, I relaxed in the shade until we were ready to leave the area.

On the drive back, we were gifted with a nice *Shamal*, a sand storm that made us pull off the road for a time. Soft, shifting, eternal sands have a certain beauty about them and assume many windblown shapes, all of them graceful.

Our visit wound down and we returned home via a nice clean Saudia plane, and I wondered which one of our friends had serviced the engines.

Another visit we made included the grand opening of the new King Khalid Airport, about twenty kilometers outside Riyadh on a new, divided highway. I went with Dan that day.

The airport is a magnificent structure with huge areas of tiled steps flowing with water, potted plants everywhere, huge and high-domed windows. Arabic arches graced every area imaginable. Escalators, very new in the Kingdom, caused consternation for some of the women. I saw a woman hesitate in fear at one, but her man shoved her on. She grabbed the rails to hang on and rode it.

One magnificent old man, at least eighty if not more, sported gray chin whiskers that jutted out like an old Biblical prophet. He walked along in his gold trimmed robe and regal Arab head dress. He proudly used his cane, leading behind him, in a row, four black-clad young wives. They either carried a tiny baby in their arms, or were obviously pregnant, a marvelous display of his fertility!

Chapter 30

The Persian Gulf

Judy took a trip to Houfuf and the Persian Gulf with Carla and two men. She said that in Houfuf, the *matawas* were so severe, they covered everything but their eyes to avoid further inspection by these religious police. It put a damper on their shopping. The town was small and rather rustic, and they managed to visit a few shops. As they never felt comfortable, they didn't linger.

Houfuf is a huge farming area, being located in one of the larger oasis areas in the Eastern Province of the country. Green fields abound, date palms, grazing cattle and goats dotted the fields. This fertile area is surrounded in every direction by endless miles of sweeping grayish sand dunes.

Nearing the Persian Gulf, oil derricks formed long lines which were thick and wide and covered more than one hundred fifty miles in length. She described those fields by saying they drove through an oil-smelling forest of working wells. The mere number of those wells were enough to stagger the imagination. It made her wonder how much oil the world requires each day.

Coming to the waters of the Persian Gulf, they decided to swim. The waters were cool and refreshing, but the four of them found it difficult to enjoy the ocean after seeing Saudi women covered head to toe in black, sitting on the beach watching their men sport about in the cool waves, while they sat upon the sand with their daughters, sweltering in the 120 degree heat.

Chapter 31

The Bedouin Camp

Sa'ad, a Bedouin man, received renal dialysis for the required one year before receiving a donor kidney from his brother. This was a universal requirement and allowed time for possible restoration of kidney function and all the testing required before the actual transplant might take place. They found a good match in his brother, Mohammed.

The transplant surgery was successful and Sa'ad eventually went home. A few months later the transplant team was invited out into the Saudi desert to visit their encampment and enjoy Bedouin hospitality as a gesture of thanks.

My friend Jamilla, who is Iraqi and American, invited me to accompany the group since she was the designated interpreter for the occasion. Delighted to be included in this chance to see a real Bedouin encampment, I readily accepted. I was eager to be a part of something I'd never thought to experience. We often sent patients home to their life in the sands and then wondered about them in so primitive an environment.

We rode out in two cars, a long way into trackless wastes where no living thing seemed to grow. Sa'ad rode in the first car as a guide to their camp.

Arriving, we were ushered to a large, clean tent, set up just for us. It was light and airy with Persian-type carpets overlaid on the sand. We also visited around the camp after the initial Arabic coffee and dates.

Their coffee seemed to be as much Cardamom seeds as actual coffee, and bitter. The men made it and observed a sort of ritual in the doing. First the coffee beans were lightly roasted in a heavy spoon shaped pan held over hot coals by a long handle then they were ground and brewed. The cardamom seeds were ground separately and brewed before the two liquids were mixed and served.

They served the bitter greenish liquid to us in tiny ornate cups. We sipped it and had a few dates with our host. He smiled his pleasure, happy to accommodate us, and beamed in delight that we enjoyed our refreshment.

Free to wander about the camp, we went too close to the men's quarters and were warned away. No females were allowed in that area, but the men were cordially invited and sat with the males for quite a while.

In the women's tent, we saw sand floors and baby goats wandering about with the small children. Our men did not enter that area either.

Surprised to see a plastic wrapped Tylenol pill half hidden in the sand, we wondered how carefully they took their prescribed medications. We saw no overweight people in that camp, men or women. It was easy to see why almost every Saudi whose cholesterol levels were checked were on the low side, usually 125 or below for total cholesterol. With my 480, I envied them that.

Sa'ad, a tall, slimly built man, who appeared to be in his forties, wore a small beard and red checkered *gutra*. I snapped a picture of the two of them bringing our dinner. They carried the heavily laden tray between them and it made a graceful picture of hospitality. Our food was served by Sa'ad and his brother, Mohammed. Each wore their *gutras* around their waist which kept the tails from dragging in the food—not a bad idea.

We were served goat meat over rice with Arabic flat bread and tomatoes set out for those who wanted them. Fruit baskets containing oranges and tangerines served as our desert. During the meal we sat on rugs in the tent provided for us. The two brothers did not join us in this meal.

Their diet has little fat. Camel milk is very rich, but the goat meat eaten is usually lean and cooked underground in a pit.

The Arabic bread is eaten without butter. It may be dipped in a *fule* bean dish, if served, or eaten with rice and meat. Salad is eaten without dressing. Cows are not generally raised in Saudi Arabia, making butter and beef more of a rarity. There are large dairy farms now, but those products weren't available to the desert dwellers that often.

After we ate, we lay about for a while to rest and chat. We thought these were the poorest of the Bedouin, since they had no camels or water trucks. Poor or not, their government paid for the medical care they received and they had as good as it was possible for us to give.

The government also flew people to other countries for treatment if that should be required for a cure. That oil money was freely spent on the little people of Saudi Arabia was a surety. We saw that often.

The government provided some things for the desert people, whether a prize or special reward such as a water truck. If they had one, it was out of our sight. Their tents were of black goat hair with a few light colored stripes woven in for décor or tribal markings. We weren't sure about the reason for it. They had lived this way for many centuries.

No local school houses were available for the formal education of Bedouin children. They had to learn their role in life from their elders. Male children were taught by men and might be sent away to schools as well. Females learned their role in life from their mothers, aunts, or other female members of the tribe. This tribe might have been very poor, but they were a proud people, too.

There were elementary, high schools, and universities scattered over the Kingdom. If any child, especially male, wished to be educated it could certainly be arranged. These were blessings provided by oil revenues, but educating females had been slow to catch on. By report, female education consisted mostly of the teachings of the Koran and female duties as required by the laws of the Muslim faith.

We spent time with the female side of the encampment, visiting in their tents and seeing them without their facial masks. Bedouin women usually cover all of their faces, except their eyes. Hair is never shown at all. The women were not masked within their quarters. They were very curious about us, certainly, but no less than we were about them.

We tried to chat with our limited Arabic and laughed frequently in the doing. Family was always important and they wanted to know if we had *waleed* or *bint.* How many sons or *waleed* did we have?

Daughters or *binti* and what were their names? It seemed they barely knew of our life at all. If they had never studied the outside world, then no wonder. They knew the doctor had saved *Sa'ad's* life, but not how it was done.

What we found amazing was the number of children with strabismus, or crossed eyes. In learning how closely they marry, it became understandable.

This was also one of the major reasons for their open heart surgeries. Most of those operations dealt with valve replacements, and rarely a clogged blood vessel.

Their clothing left much to be desired. Though the sands are very clean, clothes do get stained with food and sweat, and a good Laundromat would have been helpful. It only added to the mystery of how people had lived like that for untold centuries.

We did know that when an area became unclean from human habitation, they picked up their tents and moved to a clean area, leaving the elements to purify their last camp.

With the fierce desert heat we had already experienced, that wouldn't be a problem.

What on earth did those goats eat? We saw no blade of grass anywhere, and certainly no lush oasis lurking nearby. These people had to have had a steady supply of goods from some community, but with what could they buy amenities? The King was generous with his oil revenues, and we could only guess it trickled down to these folks, too.

We left them and climbed into our air-cooled vehicles to return to the hospital compounds we lived in. We had seen something of the romantic Arab lifestyle, tasted the food, enjoyed the friendly hospitality, and believed we were lucky people to have been born into the modern world for all its problems.

Chapter 32

Malina

Many Filipinos worked in Saudi Arabia. They were well trained and taught English from their early grades. Known as hard, productive workers, they traveled to many countries for work. Those employees recruited for work in Saudi Arabia had a certain percentage of their wages taken and sent to the Philippine government before they ever received their paychecks. Wages paid in Saudi riyals equaled five or six times their rate of pay at home and they did not complain about the extra tax.

They frequently suffered discrimination from the Arabs. Their country had less status than Britain, the United States, or Europe, and status is all to the Arab. If we were thought of as paid servants, how much more did they consider the little Filipino a servant?

We heard rumors of men dressed as police, waiting at bus stops to tell Filipino girls they had to get off the bus. If they did they get off, they were taken by these men and never seen again. Because of this, we always warned new arrivals of these rumors.

One girl said, "Because we are small and dark, they can do this?"

We could only say, "This is what we have heard."

Unable to verify the truth of such stories, we felt it was important to pass along the information. In a country where so much was hidden behind walls, where only positive things were ever told, how could we be sure of the truth? We decided to err on the side of safety.

As mentioned before, some of the Filipino ladies did prostitution, and did so at their own peril. They were there to make money for their families at home and many did what they could to earn it.

Most Filipinos we met had the hope of coming to America and had that expectation in their plans. They asked many questions, none more than the little Filipino girl who attended the princess during the time the mother, the First Wife, resided at King Faisal for her surgery. This has been mentioned previously. That little one worked like a slave for her demanding princess.

We met one Filipina who came to Riyadh as a secretary. She was hired from Manila by one of the families we knew quite well since they had a patient who rated near-royal status and could stay as long as he wanted. Malina frequently came in with the family on visits to the patient.

We often chatted with her during those times. At first, she seemed happy with her arrangement, except when she complained quietly to us. She did housework, rather than the secretarial work she was hired to do. Malina was a pretty girl, in her late twenties. She was small and delicate, with black eyes and black hair.

We thought little of her situation until Judy, Gail, and I had been invited to spend a Ramadan night at the home of this Saudi family. During this religious period, we observed the fasting rules of Ramadan in their presence and did that at work as well.

Their home was a large, three-story house surrounded with the usual eight foot walls, if not higher. A hat rack held several *egals* and *gutras* but, of course, no hats. I had to take a picture of that. The home was comfortably furnished, using large quantities of velvet covered chairs and divans. Thick Middle Eastern rugs covered the floor. In the kitchen was an American coffee maker which had never been used. It was set on the counter in such a way that we knew they had no idea how to work it. *Mr. Coffee* did not come with Arabic instructions.

The Holy month of Ramadan is from one moon to the next moon, about one month. Their calendar is the Hegira calendar which dates from July 16, 622. This calendar is 11 days shorter than our year, thus the month, Ramadan, moves 11 days back from the year before. Telling a person's age becomes more difficult because of this as well. Over a period of forty years, that person would be 440 days younger than with our system.

At work, we did not eat, drink or smoke in the presence of a Muslim from the time in the morning when one could distinguish a white thread from a black thread, all day until the sun disappeared below the horizon. Muslim workers were given shorter hours during this time. Patients observed the fast if their doctor allowed it. Women during their menses may not observe the fast, or any patient too ill. Time missed had to be made up, thus for a woman, it never could be.

We sat quietly about, conversing the best we could while waiting for the sun to disappear. At that time the fast was broken by drinking a heavy fruit drink. After that we sat around the cloth laid upon the floor and enjoyed the food. They made a dish of chopped tomatoes, cucumbers, and cilantro which we found absolutely delicious, then, roasted chicken, Arabic bread, Hummus, and more thick fruity drink. Of Malina, we saw nothing.

During that time, our host noticed us looking at the *egals* hung on the hat rack. He explained further uses for the heavy, hard, smooth, black double ring usually worn on the head. He said, "They weapon." He demonstrated how he could hit an enemy with it by whooshing it through the air. Then he said, "Can tie horse, too." He twisted it into a nice set of hobbles. The *egal* looked different after that.

That night we visited a mall none of us had ever been to, one frequented almost exclusively by Arabs. Our host played a soft jazz on his car radio, and we laughingly decided that a man who played music like that couldn't be all bad.

At the mall, he found his mother amid numerous small black shrouded females and knew her instantly. That amazed us, but everything did during that night. Women have dressed this way for centuries. For us, being in the midst of it, everything seemed so new.

That night, we slept on the floor in our clothes in a large room with his mother. Then came the morning, and we needed to get back to our compound. We went to the kitchen.

There we saw Malina, pale and crying about her situation. She said they made her stay in a room on the top floor which had no refrigeration. She was not allowed to lock her door at night. She worked at cleaning a huge iron cooking range while she spoke.

"They never intended me for secretarial work and refuse to allow me to go home until I work to pay for the return flight." She stepped outside and vomited, then hurried to clean up the vomit lest they see it.

She appeared much thinner and said she had lost a lot of weight. She frequently glanced about in fear which made us wonder if the bruises we saw on her arms meant she had been beaten. We didn't know how to comfort her and there was no one we could call, but our imaginations ran rampant at hearing her story. In my mind, because of the vomiting, I wondered if she had gotten pregnant, unwillingly, of course.

We had to get back to the compound and I was elected to find our host, awaken him, and ask him to take us back. I went up to the second floor. There were three or four rooms with closed doors. Checking all the doors, I found one that had cool air coming from beneath it.

Gingerly, I opened it and saw three men asleep on the floor. I chose the one I thought was our host and it was him. He awakened easily at my touch and came downstairs. He drove us home, and we thanked him for the wonderful Ramadan night.

Alone, we shook our heads at what we had seen, at the frustration of seeing another form of slavery and being unable to do anything about it. It was not our country. We had no power, nor anyone to turn to regarding this poor girl's plight. And this took place within a family that was well respected with high status in the Kingdom.

Some months later, we heard they had found a young Filipino woman lying dead in the street. The area seemed about right, though when you are driven everywhere, it's very hard to keep your bearings in this city. Could it have been Malina? Horrified at our thoughts, but knowing it could be true, we could only shake our heads, wondering…

Chapter 33

Maternity

Occasionally, they asked us to work in areas other than where we were assigned. This one night I worked in post-partum, not my forte, but nothing I hadn't done before. My nights there were a revelation about childbirth in the Kingdom. Many of the hospital sized beds lay covered with lavish king sized comforters to give the effect of importance and elegance to the bed's occupant. This enhanced the mother's status as much as possible. In addition, she had exotic candies and sweetmeats to hand out to her visitors when they came to see the new little Mohammed or Noura.

Nearing time for the expected visit of the child's father, the new mother would hurriedly ask for her baby and transform herself into the loving picture she wished to present. I only saw this in a few cases and found it shocking to realize she had no real interest in her new baby other than pleasing her husband and showing him what a fine mother she was.

Having a baby every year whether she wished to or not might have that effect, yet the woman had to play the part. Should he divorce her, he kept all their children, and she must have loved some of them. Once divorced, it would be unlikely she would ever be married again.

During the husband's, family members, or his mother's visits, she held and cuddled the child. As soon as they left the hospital, she gave the baby back to the staff and never saw it unless she had to feed it. One child had been the victim of this indifference.

Little Abdullah was beautiful, with extra-long, sweeping lashes. His mother had let milk run down his throat, choking him to the point he had suffered partial loss of brain function. We believed his future looked dismal indeed. The nurses told me she had no interest in the child, except during the father's visits, and had let this happen to him while baby Abdullah was held in her arms. They said she was in every year for a new birth. They felt she just didn't care anymore. Her only fear lay in displeasing the father, and she was careful to avoid that.

One of our acquaintances, on the other hand, had a happy marriage. We visited her upon the birth of her second daughter, Nouf. She sat in her bed like a queen, beautiful, with her thick long hair braided into a long plait that hung gracefully down one side of her neck. This gave us hope that some women were happy in their role as Saudi wives. She had provided two daughters so far, but we heard later, they had a son. Her husband had traveled over the world and seemed a kindly man. We thought her a lucky woman, luckier than most, and an only wife.

Some happenings on the maternity ward brought us back to the realities of a Saudi female's life, however. Nurses told us that one day a mother brought her young, unmarried daughter to the maternity ward in active labor. As the story unfolded, our blood ran cold!

It seemed the girl had accompanied her family to England during the past year and in the time there she met someone and became pregnant. The mother had carefully kept this from the girl's father until the girl went into labor. Then the secret was out. The girl was little more than fourteen years old when this happened.

The father, in a towering rage when he learned of it, stormed the labor unit wanting to take her and her newborn daughter out into the desert. His family's honor had been sullied and she had to pay the price for it. He was finally allowed to take the young girl from the hospital. They refused to allow him to take the child, maintaining that the baby was innocent. The child would go to one of his other wives. We wondered what life held for this poor infant.

Then he took his little daughter out into the desert and killed her. We know for certain, for that was the price paid when a woman was taken in sin. It was referred to as an honor killing and shocked each one of us. Again, we were powerless to do anything for this girl. One could only imagine how brutally he did this horrific deed because of his terrible rage. We tried to shut the picture from our thoughts, but it would always be ingrained in our minds and memories.

A thing like that reinforces the impression that many Saudi women rate right up there along with cattle or goats and are only useful for breeding purposes. Are they cherished? Yes, some of them were. You just had to look for the signs.

Chapter 34

Beheadings

We heard often about the beheadings which took place downtown on the courthouse steps. We looked at those steps when we were down there, but we made very sure we never went into downtown Riyadh on Fridays. Thursdays and Fridays were their week end. Friday was the holiest day and the day of the beheadings.

The names of the guilty and their crimes were published weekly in the Arab News and the Saudi Gazette, so there was no question about authenticity. The convicted had to confess their sins before two or more witness to be pronounced guilty. They readily confessed lest they face Allah with a lie upon their lips.

Angus, my Scottish friend, had a visiting engineer from New York. He wanted more than anything to see the beheadings and made a point of going downtown on Fridays. I thought it rather grim that he actually wanted to see something like that. He did and took pictures, surreptitiously, of course, which were developed outside the Kingdom. He made sure he went downtown on the highest holy day to witness the beheadings and there were usually two or more each week.

"If they see you anywhere around, they will make you stand there and watch," he told us. "You can't escape them. They have guns."

None of my acquaintances went to town on Fridays, because we didn't want to see rolling heads and spurting blood. Unlike out system in The States, it didn't take twenty years and dozens of appeals in the Saudi courts before sentence was carried out. It was done in a few short weeks or days.

One story we heard had detailed the story of a young girl who refused to marry a young man after he had offered for her hand several times. Rebuffed, the young man lay in wait for her. One day, when she came outside on an errand, he caught her and raped her. He believed she would have to marry him.

It was not to be. Her father put her to death because she had dishonored the family. The young man was beheaded because he had caused her death. It was only one of a multitude of the stories we heard while living in the kingdom.

We heard they still stone women taken in adultery, but now-a-days they put the woman in a bag and dump a truck load of rocks over her, then drive a truck over it several times to finish the deed. This was, of course, what we were told. The truth? Who knows? But it might be the more modern way to do it. They still cut off hands for theft and heads for murder as well.

Chapter 35

Saying Goodbye

After four years of no daily concerns, tires, insurance, driving a car, and all the everyday things at home, I felt ready to assume that life again. The growing distance between my children and myself tipped the balance. I did not re-new my contract and prepared for that exit-only stamp on my passport.

Judy had left a few weeks earlier, and her farewell parties, though a lot of fun, held the sad notes of goodbye to the grandest of adventures we had ever lived. Did I want that?

I shipped far too much cargo and had several good-bye parties. New faces appear as you depart. A new nurse came to the apartment and settled in. We chatted and I displayed my gold for her to see. I had a lot of it and we enjoyed looking at it, each bit reminding me of a special event in a very special place.

The floor threw me a great party. I had another one with my friends at the Thai Restaurant. DHL took my half ton of cargo, which was way up from five suitcases I had when I arrived four years ago.

Of all the goodbyes, saying goodbye to the Arab hurt the most. He spoke little English but he liked to talk with us, perhaps to sharpen what he did know. He took me to the Alkazama Hotel for coffee that last evening and took Aquila, his father's *mirafic,* along, of course. It would never have done for me to be seen with him alone.

The Arab helped us see into some of their culture, befriended us in many ways, and we believed, enjoyed the time spent with all of us as well. We had his voice on tape, and though we didn't know what he was saying, we just listen sometimes and it takes us back to the grandest adventure we'll ever know.

Ramona Forrest

Judith Corcoran

Betty & Peter

Angus & Judy

Ramona & Saudi

Ramona with Alya & Nasser

Judy & Larry

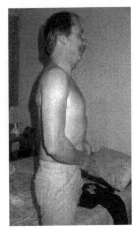

Larry

Typical group of Arab men
watching the nurses.
Hardly anyone holds a job.

After Hash, they dump thick
green stuff on each other.
It's a British thing.

Ramona & Contessa
at Orly in Paris

Kissing a cardinal

Larry at the C party

Ramona at the C party

Alya

Burned Bedouin boy

The bed was too soft.

Hey, Jude, nice back view.

Judy & Reginald
(He's supposed to be a clock)

Judy, Larry & Reginald

In the sand dunes

Ramona & Judy picking
faggah truffles

Hiding from the wicked heat

Judy on the camel trail

Dancing

Instructors at Al
Hamdullah College

Ramona & Judy

Larry & Judy

Gold-gilded pictures
in dining room

Ramona, Sheika &
Haifa al Anazi

Tea break on the way to Saudi's farm

Inside Saudi's farmhouse

After lunch with Saudi
Angus, Ramona & Judy

Latifa and her son
Abdulrahman

Judy fixing sound
for patient

The arrow on the ceiling
showing the way to Mecca
for prayer times & death

Ramona & Larry

Judy & Bedouin boy

Aguila & Ramona after
foot amalia

Sudanese men in
traditional dress

Ramona & Larry as cats

About the Authors

Ramona Forrest

Ramona Forrest is a retired RN. She keeps busy writing novels—and traveling whenever possible. Forrest has resided in the back country of Arizona, assisted in round-ups, worked in Saudi Arabia, and has had the pleasure of traveling extensively. She now resides in Phoenix and spends much time in gardening, writing, entertaining friends, and family.

Judith Corcoran

Judith Corcoran is a retired nurse who lives in the Boston area. When not writing or entertaining her large family and many friends, Corcoran spends as much time as possible at the beach. *Lifting the Veil*, a book she has co-authored with author and fellow nurse Ramona Forrest, is a about their experiences working as nurses in the Middle East.

Printed in Great Britain
by Amazon.co.uk, Ltd.,
Marston Gate.